TWO PLAYS

MACMILLAN AND CO., LIMITED
LONDON · BOMBAY · CALCUTTA · MADRAS
MELBOURNE

THE MACMILLAN COMPANY
NEW YORK · BOSTON · CHICAGO
DALLAS · SAN FRANCISCO

THE MACMILLAN CO. OF CANADA, LTD.
TORONTO

Sean O'Casey

from a portrait by Augustus John

TWO PLAYS

JUNO AND THE PAYCOCK
THE SHADOW OF A GUNMAN

BY

SEAN O'CASEY

WITH PORTRAIT OF THE AUTHOR
BY AUGUSTUS JOHN

MACMILLAN AND CO., LIMITED
ST. MARTIN'S STREET, LONDON
1927

TO

MAURA

AND TO

THE ABBEY THEATRE

CONTENTS

vii

Juno and the Paycock was first produced in the Abbey Theatre, Dublin, on March the 3rd, 1924, with the following cast:

"CAPTAIN" JACK BOYLE . . .	Barry Fitzgerald
"JUNO" BOYLE	. Sara Allgood
JOHNNY BOYLE	Arthur Shields
MARY BOYLE	Eileen Crowe
"JOXER" DALY	. F. J. McCormick
MRS. MAISIE MADIGAN . . .	. Maureen Delany
"NEEDLE" NUGENT	. Michael J. Dolan
MRS. TANCRED	. Christine Hayden
JERRY DEVINE	. P. J. Carolan
CHARLIE BENTHAM . . .	. Gabriel J. Fallon
FIRST IRREGULAR . . .	. Maurice Esmonde
SECOND IRREGULAR . . .	. Michael J. Dolan
FIRST FURNITURE REMOVER . .	. Peter Nolan
SECOND FURNITURE REMOVER .	. Tony Quinn
COAL-BLOCK VENDOR . . .	. Tony Quinn
SEWING-MACHINE MAN . .	. Peter Nolan
TWO NEIGHBOURS .	Eileen O'Kelly, Irene Murphy

JUNO AND THE PAYCOCK

A Tragedy in Three Acts

THE CHARACTERS IN THE PLAY

"CAPTAIN" JACK BOYLE.
JUNO BOYLE, *his wife.*
JOHNNY BOYLE ⎫ *their children.*
MARY BOYLE ⎭
"JOXER" DALY.
MRS. MAISIE MADIGAN.
"NEEDLE" NUGENT, *a tailor.*
MRS. TANCRED.

⎱ *Residents in the Tenement*

JERRY DEVINE.
CHARLIE BENTHAM, *a school teacher.*
AN IRREGULAR MOBILIZER.
TWO IRREGULARS.
A COAL-BLOCK VENDOR.
A SEWING MACHINE MAN.
TWO FURNITURE REMOVAL MEN.
TWO NEIGHBOURS.

SCENE

ACT I.—The living apartment of a two-roomed tenancy of the Boyle family, in a tenement house in Dublin.

ACT II.—The same.

ACT III.—The same.

A few days elapse between Acts I. and II., and two months between Acts II. and III.

During Act III. the curtain is lowered for a few minutes to denote the lapse of one hour.

Period of the play, 1922.

ACT I

*The living room of a two-room tenancy occupied by
the* BOYLE *family in a tenement house in
Dublin.   Left, a door leading to another part
of the house; left of door a window looking
into the street; at back a dresser; farther to
right at back, a window looking into the
back of the house.   Between the window and
the dresser is a picture of the Virgin; below
the picture, on a bracket, is a crimson bowl in
which a floating votive light is burning.
Farther to the right is a small bed partly
concealed by cretonne hangings strung on a
twine.   To the right is the fireplace; near
the fireplace is a door leading to the other
room.   Beside the fireplace is a box con-
taining coal.   On the mantelshelf is an
alarm clock lying on its face.   In a corner
near the window looking into the back is a
galvanized bath.   A table and some chairs.
On the table are breakfast things for one.   A*

3

*teapot is on the hob and a frying-pan stands
inside the fender.   There are a few books
on the dresser and one on the table.   Leaning
against   the   dresser   is   a   long-handled
shovel — the   kind   invariably   used   by
labourers   when   turning   concrete   or   mixing
mortar.   JOHNNY BOYLE is sitting crouched
beside the fire.   MARY with her jumper off—
it is lying on the back of a chair—is arranging
her hair before a tiny mirror perched on the
table.   Beside the mirror is stretched out the
morning paper which she looks at when she
isn't gazing into the mirror.   She is a well-
made and good-looking girl of twenty-two.
Two forces are working in her mind—one,
through the circumstances of her life, pulling
her back; the other, through the influence of
books she has read, pushing her forward.
The opposing forces are apparent in her
speech and her manners, both of which are
degraded by her environment, and improved
by her acquaintance—slight though it be—
with literature.   The time is early forenoon.*

MARY (*looking at the paper*). On a little bye-
road, out beyant Finglas, he was found.

    (MRS. BOYLE *enters by door on right; she
    has been shopping and carries a small*

4

parcel in her hand. She is forty-five years of age, and twenty years ago she must have been a pretty woman; but her face has now assumed that look which ultimately settles down upon the faces of the women of the working-class; a look of listless monotony and harassed anxiety, blending with an expression of mechanical resistance. Were circumstances favourable, she would probably be a handsome, active and clever woman.)

MRS. BOYLE. Isn't he come in yet?

MARY. No, mother.

MRS. BOYLE. Oh, he'll come in when he likes; struttin' about the town like a paycock with Joxer, I suppose. I hear all about Mrs. Tancred's son is in this mornin's paper.

MARY. The full details are in it this mornin'; seven wounds he had—one entherin' the neck, with an exit wound beneath the left shoulder-blade; another in the left breast penethratin' the heart, an' . . .

JOHNNY (*springing up from the fire*). Oh, quit that readin', for God's sake! Are yous losin' all your feelins? It'll soon be that none of yous'll read anythin' that's not about butcherin'!

(*He goes quickly into the room on left.*)

5

MARY. He's gettin' very sensitive, all of a sudden!

MRS. BOYLE. I'll read it myself, Mary, by an' by, when I come home. Everybody's sayin' that he was a Die-hard—thanks be to God that Johnny had nothin' to do with him this long time. . . . (*Opening the parcel and taking out some sausages, which she places on a plate*) Ah, then, if that father o' yours doesn't come in soon for his breakfast, he may go without any; I'll not wait much longer for him.

MARY. Can't you let him get it himself when he comes in?

MRS. BOYLE. Yes, an' let him bring in Joxer Daly along with him? Ay, that's what he'd like, an' that's what he's waitin' for—till he thinks I'm gone to work, an' then sail in with the boul' Joxer, to burn all the coal an' dhrink all the tea in the place, to show them what a good Samaritan he is! But I'll stop here till he comes in, if I have to wait till to-morrow mornin'.

VOICE OF JOHNNY INSIDE. Mother!

MRS. BOYLE. Yis?

VOICE OF JOHNNY. Bring us in a dhrink o' wather.

MRS. BOYLE. Bring in that fella a dhrink o' wather, for God's sake, Mary.

6

MARY. Isn't he big an' able enough to come out an' get it himself?

MRS. BOYLE. If you weren't well yourself you'd like somebody to bring you in a dhrink o' wather.   (*She brings in drink and returns.*)

MRS. BOYLE. Isn't it terrible to have to be waitin' this way! You'd think he was bringin' twenty pouns a week into the house the way he's going on. He wore out the Health Insurance long ago, he's afther wearin' out the unemployment dole, an', now, he's thryin' to wear out me! An' constantly singin', no less, when he ought always to be on his knees offerin' up a Novena for a job!

MARY (*tying a ribbon, fillet wise around her head*). I don't like this ribbon, ma; I think I'll wear the green—it looks betther than the blue.

MRS. BOYLE. Ah, wear whatever ribbon you like, girl, only don't be botherin' me. I don't know what a girl on strike wants to be wearin' a ribbon round her head for or silk stockins on her legs either; its wearin' them things that make the employers think they're givin' yous too much money.

MARY. The hour is past now when we'll ask the employers' permission to wear what we like.

MRS. BOYLE. I don't know why you wanted to walk out for Jennie Claffey; up to this you never had a good word for her.

MARY. What's the use of belongin' to a Trades Union if you won't stand up for your principles? Why did they sack her? It was a clear case of victimization. We couldn't let her walk the streets, could we?

MRS. BOYLE. No, of course yous couldn't— yous wanted to keep her company. Wan victim wasn't enough. When the employers sacrifice wan victim, the Trades Unions go wan betther be sacrificin' a hundred.

MARY. It doesn't matther what you say, ma—a principle's a principle.

MRS. BOYLE. Yis; an' when I go into oul' Murphy's to-morrow, an' he gets to know that, instead o' payin' all, I'm goin' to borry more, what'll he say when I tell him a principle's a principle? What'll we do if he refuses to give us any more on tick?

MARY. He daren't refuse—if he does, can't you tell him he's paid?

MRS. BOYLE. It's lookin' as if he was paid, whether he refuses or no.

(JOHNNY *appears at the door on left. He can be plainly seen now; he is a thin delicate fellow, something younger*
8

than MARY. *He has evidently gone through a rough time. His face is pale and drawn; there is a tremulous look of indefinite fear in his eyes. The left sleeve of his coat is empty, and he walks with a slight halt.*)

JOHNNY. I was lyin' down; I thought yous were gone. Oul' Simon Mackay is thrampin' about like a horse over me head, an' I can't sleep with him—they're like thunder-claps in me brain! The curse o'—God forgive me for goin' to curse!

MRS. BOYLE. There, now; go back an' lie down agen, an I'll bring you in a nice cup o' tay.

JOHNNY. Tay, tay, tay! You're always thinkin' o' tay. If a man was dyin', you'd thry to make him swally a cup o' tay!

(He goes back.)

MRS. BOYLE. I don't know what's goin' to be done with him. The bullet he got in the hip in Easter Week was bad enough, but the bomb that shatthered his arm in the fight in O'Connell Street put the finishin' touch on him. I knew he was makin' a fool of himself. God knows I went down on me bended knees to him not to go agen the Free State.

MARY. He stuck to his principles, an', no

9

matther how you may argue, ma, a principle's a principle.

VOICE OF JOHNNY. Is Mary goin' to stay here?

MARY. No, I'm not goin' to stay here; you can't expect me to be always at your beck an' call, can you?

VOICE OF JOHNNY. I won't stop here be meself!

MRS. BOYLE. Amn't I nicely handicapped with the whole o' yous! I don't know what any o' yous ud do without your ma. (*To* JOHNNY) Your father'll be here in a minute, an' if you want anythin', he'll get it for you.

JOHNNY. I hate assin' him for anythin'. . . . He hates to be assed to stir. . . . Is the light lightin' before the picture o' the Virgin?

MRS. BOYLE. Yis, yis! The wan inside to St. Anthony isn't enough, but he must have another wan to the Virgin here!

> (JERRY DEVINE *enters hastily. He is about twenty-five, well set, active and earnest. He is a type, becoming very common now in the Labour Movement, of a mind knowing enough to make the mass of his associates, who know less, a power, and too little to broaden that power for the benefit of all.* MARY

seizes her jumper and runs hastily into room left.)

JERRY (*breathless*). Where's the Captain, Mrs. Boyle, where's the Captain?

MRS. BOYLE. You may well ass a body that: he's wherever Joxer Daly is—dhrinkin' in some snug or another.

JERRY. Father Farrell is just afther stoppin' to tell me to run up an' get him to go to the new job that's goin' on in Rathmines; his cousin is foreman o' the job, an' Father Farrell was speakin' to him about poor Johnny an' his father bein' idle so long, an' the foreman told Father Farrell to send the Captain up an' he'd give him a start—I wondher where I'd find him?

MRS. BOYLE. You'll find he's ayther in Ryan's or Foley's.

JERRY. I'll run round to Ryan's—I know it's a great house o' Joxer's.   (*He rushes out.*)

MRS. BOYLE (*piteously*). There now, he'll miss that job, or I know for what! If he gets win' o' the word, he'll not come back till evenin', so that it'll be too late. There'll never be any good got out o' him so long as he goes with that shouldher-shruggin' Joxer. I killin' meself workin', an' he sthruttin' about from mornin' till night like a paycock!

(The steps of two persons are heard coming up a flight of stairs. They are the footsteps of CAPTAIN BOYLE *and* JOXER. CAPTAIN BOYLE *is singing in a deep, sonorous, self-honouring voice.)*

THE CAPTAIN. Sweet Spirit, hear me prayer! Hear . . . oh . . . hear . . . me prayer . . . hear, oh, hear . . . Oh, he . . . ar . . . oh, he . . . ar . . . me . . . pray . . . er!

JOXER *(outside)*. Ah, that's a darlin' song, a daaarlin' song!

MRS. BOYLE *(viciously)*. Sweet spirit hear his prayer! Ah, then, I'll take me solemn affey-davey, it's not for a job he's prayin'!

(She sits down on the bed so that the cretonne hangings hide her from the view of those entering.)

*(*THE CAPTAIN *comes slowly in. He is a man of about sixty; stout, grey-haired and stocky. His neck is short, and his head looks like a stone ball that one sometimes sees on top of a gate-post. His cheeks, reddish-purple, are puffed out, as if he were always repressing an almost irrepressible ejaculation. On his upper lip is a crisp, tightly cropped moustache; he carries himself with the upper part of his body slightly thrown*

back, and his stomach slightly thrust forward. His walk is a slow, consequential strut. His clothes are dingy, and he wears a faded seaman's cap with a glazed peak.)

BOYLE (*to* JOXER, *who is still outside*). Come on, come on in, Joxer; she's gone out long ago, man. If there's nothing else to be got, we'll furrage out a cup o' tay, anyway. It's the only bit I get in comfort when she's away. 'Tisn't Juno should be her pet name at all, but Deirdre of the Sorras, for she's always grousin'.

(JOXER *steps cautiously into the room. He may be younger than* THE CAPTAIN *but he looks a lot older. His face is like a bundle of crinkled paper; his eyes have a cunning twinkle; he is spare and loosely built; he has a habit of constantly shrugging his shoulders with a peculiar twitching movement, meant to be ingratiating. His face is invariably ornamented with a grin.)*

JOXER. It's a terrible thing to be tied to a woman that's always grousin'. I don't know how you stick it—it ud put years on me. It's a good job she has to be so ofen away, for (*with a shrug*) when the cat's away, the mice can play!

BOYLE (*with a commanding and complacent gesture*). Pull over to the fire, Joxer, an' we'll have a cup o' tay in a minute.

JOXER. Ah, a cup o' tay's a darlin' thing, a daaarlin' thing—the cup that cheers but doesn't . . .

> (JOXER'S *rhapsody is cut short by the sight of* JUNO *coming forward and confronting the two cronies. Both are stupefied.*)

MRS. BOYLE (*with sweet irony—poking the fire, and turning her head to glare at* JOXER). Pull over to the fire, Joxer Daly, an' we'll have a cup o' tay in a minute! Are you sure, now, you wouldn't like an egg?

JOXER. I can't stop, Mrs. Boyle; I'm in a desperate hurry, a desperate hurry.

MRS. BOYLE. Pull over to the fire, Joxer Daly; people is always far more comfortabler here than they are in their own place.

> (JOXER *makes hastily for the door.* BOYLE *stirs to follow him; thinks of something to relieve the situation—stops, and says suddenly*)

Joxer!

JOXER (*at door ready to bolt*). Yis?

BOYLE. You know the foreman o' that job that's goin' on down in Killesther, don't you, Joxer?

JOXER (*puzzled*). Foreman—Killesther?

BOYLE (*with a meaning look*). He's a butty o' yours, isn't he?

JOXER (*the truth dawning on him*). The foreman at Killesther—oh yis, yis. He's an oul' butty o' mine—oh, he's a darlin' man, a daarlin' man.

BOYLE. Oh, then, it's a sure thing. It's a pity we didn't go down at breakfast first thing this mornin'—we might ha' been working now; but you didn't know it then.

JOXER (*with a shrug*). It's betther late than never.

BOYLE. It's nearly time we got a start, anyhow; I'm fed up knockin' round, doin' nothin'. He promised you — gave you the straight tip?

JOXER. Yis. "Come down on the blow o' dinner," says he, "an' I'll start you, an' any friend you like to brin' with you." Ah, says I, you're a darlin' man, a daaarlin' man.

BOYLE. Well, it couldn't come at a betther time—we're a long time waitin' for it.

JOXER. Indeed we were; but it's a long lane that has no turnin'.

BOYLE. The blow up for dinner is at one— wait till I see what time it 'tis. (*He goes over to the mantelpiece, and gingerly lifts the clock.*)

MRS. BOYLE. Min' now, how you go on fiddlin' with that clock—you know the least little thing sets it asthray.

BOYLE. The job couldn't come at a betther time; I'm feelin' in great fettle, Joxer. I'd hardly believe I ever had a pain in me legs, an' last week I was nearly crippled with them.

JOXER. That's betther an' betther; ah, God never shut wan door but he opened another!

BOYLE. It's only eleven o'clock; we've lashins o' time. I'll slip on me oul' moleskins afther breakfast, an' we can saunther down at our ayse. (*Putting his hand on the shovel*) I think, Joxer, we'd betther bring our shovels?

JOXER. Yis, Captain, yis; it's betther to go fully prepared an' ready for all eventualities. You bring your long-tailed shovel, an' I'll bring me navvy. We mighten' want them, an', then agen, we might: for want of a nail the shoe was lost, for want of a shoe the horse was lost, an' for want of a horse the man was lost—aw, that's a darlin' proverb, a daarlin' . . .

(*As* JOXER *is finishing his sentence,* MRS. BOYLE *approaches the door and* JOXER *retreats hurriedly. She shuts the door with a bang.*)

BOYLE (*suggestively*). We won't be long

16

pullin' ourselves together agen when I'm working for a few weeks.

(MRS. BOYLE *takes no notice*.)

BOYLE. The foreman on the job is an oul' butty o' Joxer's; I have an idea that I know him meself. (*Silence*) . . . There's a button off the back o' me moleskin trousers. . . . If you leave out a needle an' thread I'll sew it on meself. . . . Thanks be to God, the pains in me legs is gone, anyhow!

MRS. BOYLE (*with a burst*). Look here, Mr. Jacky Boyle, them yarns won't go down with Juno. I know you an' Joxer Daly of an oul' date, an', if you think you're able to come it over me with them fairy tales, you're in the wrong shop.

BOYLE (*coughing subduedly to relieve the tenseness of the situation*). U-u-u-ugh!

MRS. BOYLE. Butty o' Joxer's! Oh, you'll do a lot o' good as long as you continue to be a butty o' Joxer's!

BOYLE. U-u-u-ugh!

MRS. BOYLE. Shovel! Ah, then, me boyo, you'd do far more work with a knife an' fork than ever you'll do with a shovel! If there was e'er a genuine job goin' you'd be dh'other way about—not able to lift your arms with the pains in your legs! Your poor wife slavin'

17   C

to keep the bit in your mouth, an' you gallivantin' about all the day like a paycock!

BOYLE. It ud be betther for a man to be
dead, betther for a man to be dead.

MRS. BOYLE (*ignoring the interruption*). Everybody callin' you " Captain ", an' you only wanst
on the wather, in an oul' collier from here to
Liverpool, when anybody, to listen or look at
you, ud take you for a second Christo For
Columbus!

BOYLE. Are you never goin' to give us a
rest?

MRS. BOYLE. Oh, you're never tired o'
lookin' for a rest.

BOYLE. D'ye want to dhrive me out o' the
house?

MRS. BOYLE. It ud be easier to dhrive you
out o' the house than to dhrive you into a job.
Here, sit down an' take your breakfast—it may
be the last you'll get, for I don't know where
the next is goin' to come from.

BOYLE. If I get this job we'll be all right.

MRS. BOYLE. Did ye see Jerry Devine?

BOYLE (*testily*). No, I didn't see him.

MRS. BOYLE. No, but you seen Joxer. Well,
he was here lookin' for you.

BOYLE. Well, let him look!

MRS. BOYLE. Oh, indeed, he may well look,

18

for it ud be hard for him to see you, an' you stuck in Ryan's snug.

BOYLE. I wasn't in Ryan's snug—I don't go into Ryan's.

MRS. BOYLE. Oh, is there a mad dog there? Well, if you weren't in Ryan's you were in Foley's.

BOYLE. I'm telling you for the last three weeks I haven't tasted a dhrop of intoxicatin' liquor. I wasn't in ayther wan snug or dh'other—I could swear that on a prayer-book—I'm as innocent as the child unborn!

MRS. BOYLE. Well, if you'd been in for your breakfast you'd ha' seen him.

BOYLE (*suspiciously*). What does he want me for?

MRS. BOYLE. He'll be back any minute an' then you'll soon know.

BOYLE. I'll dhrop out an' see if I can meet him.

MRS. BOYLE. You'll sit down an' take your breakfast, an' let me go to me work, for I'm an hour late already waitin' for you.

BOYLE. You needn't ha' waited, for I'll take no breakfast—I've a little spirit left in me still!

MRS. BOYLE. Are you goin' to have your breakfast—yes or no?

BOYLE (*too proud to yield*). I'll have no breakfast—yous can keep your breakfast. (*Plaintively*) I'll knock out a bit somewhere, never fear.

MRS. BOYLE. Nobody's goin' to coax you—don't think that. (*She vigorously replaces the pan and the sausages in the press.*)

BOYLE. I've a little spirit left in me still.

(JERRY DEVINE *enters hastily.*)

JERRY. Oh, here you are at last! I've been searchin' for you everywhere. The foreman in Foley's told me you hadn't left the snug with Joxer ten minutes before I went in.

MRS. BOYLE. An' he swearin' on the holy prayer-book that he wasn't in no snug!

BOYLE (*to* JERRY). What business is it o' yours whether I was in a snug or no? What do you want to be gallopin' about afther me for? Is a man not to be allowed to leave his house for a minute without havin' a pack o' spies, pimps an' informers cantherin' at his heels?

JERRY. Oh, you're takin' a wrong view of it, Mr. Boyle; I simply was anxious to do you a good turn. I have a message for you from Father Farrell: he says that if you go to the job that's on in Rathmines, an' ask for Foreman Mangan, you'll get a start.

BOYLE. That's all right, but I don't want the motions of me body to be watched the way an asthronomer ud watch a star. If you're folleyin' Mary aself, you've no pereeogative to be folleyin' me. (*Suddenly catching his thigh*) U-ugh, I'm afther gettin' a terrible twinge in me right leg!

MRS. BOYLE. Oh, it won't be very long now till it travels into your left wan. It's miraculous that whenever he scents a job in front of him, his legs begin to fail him! Then, me bucko, if you lose this chance, you may go an' furrage for yourself!

JERRY. This job'll last for some time too, Captain, an' as soon as the foundations are in, it'll be cushy enough.

BOYLE. Won't it be a climbin' job? How d'ye expect me to be able to go up a ladder with these legs? An', if I get up aself, how am I goin' to get down agen?

MRS. BOYLE (*viciously*). Get wan o' the labourers to carry you down in a hod! You can't climb a laddher, but you can skip like a goat into a snug!

JERRY. I wouldn't let meself be let down that easy, Mr. Boyle; a little exercise, now, might do you all the good in the world.

BOYLE. It's a docthor you should have been,

Devine—maybe you know more about the pains in me legs than meself that has them?

JERRY (*irritated*). Oh, I know nothin' about the pains in your legs; I've brought the message that Father Farrell gave me, an' that's all I can do.

MRS. BOYLE. Here, sit down an' take your breakfast, an' go an' get ready; an' don't be actin' as if you couldn't pull a wing out of a dead bee.

BOYLE. I want no breakfast, I tell you; it ud choke me afther all that's been said.   I've a little spirit left in me still.

MRS. BOYLE. Well, let's see your spirit, then, an' go in at wanst an' put on your moleskin trousers!

BOYLE (*moving towards the door on left*). It ud be bether for a man to be dead!   U-ugh! There's another twinge in me other leg! Nobody but meself knows the sufferin' I'm goin' through with the pains in these legs o' mine!

(*He goes into the room on left as* MARY *comes out with her hat in her hand.*)

MRS. BOYLE. I'll have to push off now, for I'm terrible late already, but I was determined to stay an' hunt that Joxer this time.

(*She goes off.*)

JERRY. Are you going out, Mary?

MARY. It looks like it when I'm putting on my hat, doesn't it?

JERRY. The bitther word agen, Mary.

MARY. You won't allow me to be friendly with you; if I thry, you deliberately misundherstand it.

JERRY. I didn't always misundherstand it; you were ofen delighted to have the arms of Jerry around you.

MARY. If you go on talkin' like this, Jerry Devine, you'll make me hate you!

JERRY. Well, let it be either a weddin' or a wake! Listen, Mary, I'm standin' for the Secretaryship of our Union. There's only one opposin' me; I'm popular with all the men, an' a good speaker—all are sayin' that I'll get elected.

MARY. Well?

JERRY. The job's worth three hundred an' fifty pounds a year, Mary. You an' I could live nice an' cosily on that; it would lift you out o' this place an' . . .

MARY. I haven't time to listen to you now— I have to go.

    (*She is going out when* JERRY *bars the way*.)

JERRY (*appealingly*). Mary, what's come

over you with me for the last few weeks? You
hardly speak to me, an' then only a word with
a face o' bittherness on it. Have you forgotten,
Mary, all the happy evenins that were as sweet
as the scented hawthorn that sheltered the sides
o' the road as we saunthered through the
country?

MARY. That's all over now. When you
get your new job, Jerry, you won't be long
findin' a girl far betther than I am for your
sweetheart.

JERRY. Never, never, Mary! No matther
what happens, you'll always be the same to
me.

MARY. I must be off; please let me go,
Jerry.

JERRY. I'll go a bit o' the way with you.

MARY. You needn't, thanks; I want to be
by meself.

JERRY (*catching her arm*). You're goin' to
meet another fella; you've clicked with some
one else, me lady!

MARY. That's no concern o' yours, Jerry
Devine; let me go!

JERRY. I saw yous comin' out o' the Corn-
flower Dance Class, an' you hangin' on his
arm—a thin, lanky strip of a Micky Dazzler,
with a walkin'-stick an' gloves!

VOICE OF JOHNNY (*loudly*). What are you doin' there—pullin' about everything!

VOICE OF BOYLE (*loudly and viciously*). I'm puttin' on me moleskin trousers!

MARY. You're hurtin' me arm! Let me go, or I'll scream, an' then you'll have the oul' fella out on top of us!

JERRY. Don't be so hard on a fella, Mary, don't be so hard.

BOYLE (*appearing at the door*). What's the meanin' of all this hillabaloo?

MARY. Let me go, let me go!

BOYLE. D'ye hear me—what's all this hillabaloo about?

JERRY (*plaintively*). Will you not give us one kind word, one kind word, Mary?

BOYLE. D'ye hear me talkin' to yous? What's all this hillabaloo for?

JERRY. Let me kiss your hand, your little, tiny, white hand!

BOYLE. Your little, tiny, white hand—are you takin' leave o' your senses, man?

(MARY *breaks away and rushes out.*)

BOYLE. This is nice goins on in front of her father!

JERRY. Ah, dhry up, for God's sake! (*He follows* MARY.)

BOYLE. Chiselurs don't care a damn now

about their parents, they're bringin' their fathers' grey hairs down with sorra to the grave, an' laughin' at it, laughin' at it. Ah, I suppose it's just the same everywhere—the whole worl's in a state o' chassis! (*He sits by the fire*) Breakfast! Well, they can keep their breakfast for me. Not if they went down on their bended knees would I take it—I'll show them I've a little spirit left in me still! (*He goes over to the press, takes out a plate and looks at it*) Sassige! Well, let her keep her sassige. (*He returns to the fire, takes up the teapot and gives it a gentle shake*) The tea's wet right enough. (*A pause; he rises, goes to the press, takes out the sausage, puts it on the pan, and puts both on the fire. He attends the sausage with a fork.*)

BOYLE (*singing*):

When the robins nest agen,
And the flowers are in bloom,
When the Springtime's sunny smile seems to banish
    all sorrow an' gloom;
Then me bonny blue-ey'd lad, if me heart be true till
    then—
He's promised he'll come back to me,
When the robins nest agen!

> (*He lifts his head at the high note, and then drops his eyes to the pan.*)

26

BOYLE (*singing*):

When the . . .

> (*Steps are heard approaching; he whips
> the pan off the fire and puts it under
> the bed, then sits down at the fire.   The
> door opens and a bearded man looking
> in says*):

You don't happen to want a sewin' machine?

BOYLE (*furiously*). No, I don't want e'er a
sewin' machine!

> (*He returns the pan to the fire, and
> commences to sing again.*)

BOYLE (*singing*):

When the robins nest agen,
And the flowers they are in bloom,
He's . . .

> (*A thundering knock is heard at the street
> door.*)

BOYLE. There's a terrible tatheraraa—that's
a stranger—that's nobody belongin' to the
house.   (*Another loud knock.*)

JOXER (*sticking his head in at the door*). Did
ye hear them tatherarahs?

BOYLE. Well, Joxer, I'm not deaf.

JOHNNY (*appearing in his shirt and trousers
at the door on left; his face is anxious and his
voice is tremulous*). Who's that at the door;

who's that at the door? Who gave that knock—d'ye yous hear me—are yous deaf or dhrunk or what?

BOYLE (*to* JOHNNY). How the hell do I know who 'tis? Joxer, stick your head out o' the window an' see.

JOXER. An' mebbe get a bullet in the kisser? Ah, none o' them thricks for Joxer! It's betther to be a coward than a corpse!

BOYLE (*looking cautiously out of the window*). It's a fella in a thrench coat.

JOHNNY. Holy Mary, Mother o' God, I . . .

BOYLE. He's goin' away—he must ha' got tired knockin'.

(JOHNNY *returns to the room on left.*)

BOYLE. Sit down an' have a cup o' tay, Joxer.

JOXER. I'm afraid the missus ud pop in on us agen before we'd know where we are. Somethins tellin' me to go at wanst.

BOYLE. Don't be superstitious, man; we're Dublin men, an' not boyos that's only afther comin' up from the bog o' Allen—though if she did come in, right enough, we'd be caught like rats in a thrap.

JOXER. An' you know the sort she is—she wouldn't listen to reason—an' wanse bitten twice shy.

28

BOYLE (*going over to the window at back*). If the worst came to the worst, you could dart out here, Joxer; it's only a dhrop of a few feet to the roof of the return room, an' the first minute she goes into dh'other room, I'll give you the bend, an' you can slip in an' away.

JOXER (*yielding to the temptation*). Ah, I won't stop very long anyhow. (*Picking up a book from the table*) Who's is the buk?

BOYLE. Aw, one o' Mary's; she's always readin' lately—nothin' but thrash, too. There's one I was lookin' at dh'other day: three stories, The Doll's House, Ghosts, an' The Wild Duck —buks only fit for chiselurs!

JOXER. Didja ever rade *Elizabeth, or Th' Exile o' Sibayria* . . . ah, it's a darlin' story, a daarlin' story!

BOYLE. You eat your sassige, an' never min' *Th' Exile o' Sibayria.*

(*Both sit down;* BOYLE *fills out tea, pours gravy on* JOXER's *plate, and keeps the sausage for himself.*)

JOXER. What are you wearin' your moleskin trousers for?

BOYLE. I have to go to a job, Joxer. Just afther you'd gone, Devine kem runnin' in to tell us that Father Farrell said if I went down to the job that's goin' on in Rathmines I'd get a start.

JOXER. Be the holy, that's good news!

BOYLE. How is it good news? I wondher if you were in my condition, would you call it good news?

JOXER. I thought . . .

BOYLE. You thought! You think too sudden sometimes, Joxer. D'ye know, I'm hardly able to crawl with the pains in me legs!

JOXER. Yis, yis; I forgot the pains in your legs. I know you can do nothin' while they're at you.

BOYLE. You forgot; I don't think any of yous realize the state I'm in with the pains in me legs. What ud happen if I had to carry a bag o' cement?

JOXER. Ah, any man havin' the like of them pains id be down an' out, down an' out.

BOYLE. I wouldn't mind if he had said it to meself; but, no, oh no, he rushes in an' shouts it out in front o' Juno, an' you know what Juno is, Joxer. We all know Devine knows a little more than the rest of us, but he doesn't act as if he did; he's a good boy, sober, able to talk an' all that, but still . . .

JOXER. Oh ay; able to argufy, but still . . .

BOYLE. If he's runnin' afther Mary, aself, he's not goin' to be runnin' afther me. Captain Boyle's able to take care of himself. Afther all, I'm not gettin' brought up on Virol. I never heard him usin' a curse; I don't believe he was ever dhrunk in his life—sure he's not like a Christian at all!

JOXER. You're afther takin' the word out o' me mouth—afther all, a Christian's natural, but he's unnatural.

BOYLE. His oul' fella was just the same—a Wicklow man.

JOXER. A Wicklow man! That explains the whole thing. I've met many a Wicklow man in me time, but I never met wan that was any good.

BOYLE. "Father Farrell," says he, "sent me down to tell you." Father Farrell! . . . D'ye know, Joxer, I never like to be beholden to any o' the clergy.

JOXER. It's dangerous, right enough.

BOYLE. If they do anything for you, they'd want you to be livin' in the Chapel. . . . I'm goin' to tell you somethin', Joxer, that I wouldn't tell to anybody else—the clergy always had too much power over the people in this unfortunate country.

JOXER. You could sing that if you had an air to it!

BOYLE (*becoming enthusiastic*). Didn't they prevent the people in "'47" from seizin' the

corn, an' they starvin'; didn't they down
Parnell; didn't they say that hell wasn't hot
enough nor eternity long enough to punish
the Fenians? We don't forget, we don't forget
them things, Joxer. If they've taken everything else from us, Joxer, they've left us our
memory.

JOXER (*emotionally*). For mem'ry's the only
friend that grief can call its own, that grief . . .
can . . . call . . . its own!

BOYLE. Father Farrell's beginnin' to take
a great intherest in Captain Boyle; because of
what Johnny did for his country, says he to
me wan day. It's a curious way to reward
Johnny be makin' his poor oul' father work.
But, that's what the clergy want, Joxer—work,
work, work for me an' you; havin' us mulin'
from mornin' till night, so that they may be in
betther fettle when they come hoppin' round
for their dues! Job! Well, let him give his
job to wan of his hymn-singin', prayer-spoutin',
craw-thumpin' Confraternity men!

(*The voice of a coal-block vendor is heard
chanting in the street.*)

VOICE OF COAL VENDOR. Blocks . . . coal-
blocks! Blocks . . . coal-blocks!

JOXER. God be with the young days when
you were steppin' the deck of a manly ship, with

32

the win' blowin' a hurricane through the masts, an' the only sound you'd hear was, " Port your helm! " an' the only answer, " Port it is, sir! "

BOYLE. Them was days, Joxer, them was days. Nothin' was too hot or too heavy for me then. Sailin' from the Gulf o' Mexico to the Antanartic Ocean. I seen things, I seen things, Joxer, that no mortal man should speak about that knows his Catechism. Ofen, an' ofen, when I was fixed to the wheel with a marlinspike, an' the wins blowin' fierce an' the waves lashin' an' lashin', till you'd think every minute was goin' to be your last, an' it blowed, an' blowed—blew is the right word, Joxer, but blowed is what the sailors use. . . .

JOXER. Aw, it's a darlin' word, a daarlin' word.

BOYLE. An', as it blowed an' blowed, I ofen looked up at the sky an' assed meself the question—what is the stars, what is the stars?

VOICE OF COAL VENDOR. Any blocks, coal-blocks; blocks, coal-blocks!

JOXER. Ah, that's the question, that's the question—what is the stars?

BOYLE. An' then, I'd have another look, an' I'd ass meself—what is the moon?

JOXER. Ah, that's the question—what is the moon, what is the moon?

(*Rapid steps are heard coming towards the
    door.* BOYLE *makes desperate efforts
    to hide everything;* JOXER *rushes to the
    window in a frantic effort to get out;*
    BOYLE *begins to innocently lilt "Oh, me
    darlin' Jennie, I will be thrue to thee",
    when the door is opened, and the black
    face of the* COAL VENDOR *appears.*)

THE COAL VENDOR. D'yes want any blocks?

BOYLE (*with a roar*). No, we don't want any
blocks!

JOXER (*coming back with a sigh of relief*).
That's afther puttin' the heart across me—I
could ha' sworn it was Juno. I'd betther be
goin', Captain; you couldn't tell the minute
Juno'd hop in on us.

BOYLE. Let her hop in; we may as well
have it out first as at last. I've made up me
mind—I'm not goin' to do only what she damn
well likes.

JOXER. Them sentiments does you credit,
Captain; I don't like to say anything as between
man an' wife, but I say as a butty, as a butty,
Captain, that you've stuck it too long, an' that
it's about time you showed a little spunk.

How can a man die betther than facin' fearful odds,
For th' ashes of his fathers an' the temples of his
    gods.

34

BOYLE. She has her rights—there's no one denyin' it, but haven't I me rights too?

JOXER. Of course you have—the sacred rights o' man!

BOYLE. To-day, Joxer, there's goin' to be issued a proclamation be me, establishin' an independent Republic, an' Juno'll have to take an oath of allegiance.

JOXER. Be firm, be firm, Captain; the first few minutes'll be the worst :—if you gently touch a nettle it'll sting you for your pains; grasp it like a lad of mettle, an' as soft as silk remains!

VOICE OF JUNO OUTSIDE. Can't stop, Mrs. Madigan—I haven't a minute!

JOXER (*flying out of the window*). Holy God, here she is!

BOYLE (*packing the things away with a rush in the press*). I knew that fella ud stop till she was in on top of us! (*He sits down by the fire.*)

(JUNO *enters hastily; she is flurried and excited.*)

JUNO. Oh, you're in—you must have been only afther comin' in?

BOYLE. No, I never went out.

JUNO. It's curious, then, you never heard the knockin'.

(*She puts her coat and hat on bed.*)

BOYLE. Knockin'? Of course I heard the knockin'.

JUNO. An' why didn't you open the door, then? I suppose you were so busy with Joxer that you hadn't time.

BOYLE. I haven't seen Joxer since I seen him before. Joxer! What ud bring Joxer here?

JUNO. D'ye mean to tell me that the pair of yous wasn't collogin' together here when me back was turned?

BOYLE. What ud we be collogin' together about? I have somethin' else to think of besides collogin' with Joxer. I can swear on all the holy prayer-books . . .

MRS. BOYLE. That you weren't in no snug! Go on in at wanst now, an' take off that mole-skin trousers o' yours, an' put on a collar an' tie to smarten yourself up a bit. There's a visitor comin' with Mary in a minute, an' he has great news for you.

BOYLE. A job, I suppose; let us get wan first before we start lookin' for another.

MRS. BOYLE. That's the thing that's able to put the win' up you. Well, it's no job, but news that'll give you the chance o' your life.

BOYLE. What's all the mysthery about?

MRS. BOYLE. G'win an take off the moleskin trousers when you're told!

> (BOYLE *goes into room on left.*)
>
> (MRS. BOYLE *tidies up the room, puts the shovel under the bed, and goes to the press.*)

MRS. BOYLE. Oh, God bless us, looka the way everything's thrun about!   Oh, Joxer was here, Joxer was here!

> (MARY *enters with* CHARLIE BENTHAM; *he is a young man of twenty-five, tall, good-looking, with a very high opinion of himself generally.   He is dressed in a brown coat, brown knee-breeches, grey stockings, a brown sweater, with a deep blue tie; he carries gloves and a walking-stick.*)

MRS. BOYLE (*fussing round*). Come in, Mr. Bentham; sit down, Mr. Bentham, in this chair; it's more comfortabler than that, Mr. Bentham. Himself'll be here in a minute; he's just takin' off his trousers.

MARY. Mother!

BENTHAM. Please don't put yourself to any trouble, Mrs. Boyle—I'm quite all right here, thank you.

MRS. BOYLE. An' to think of you knowin' Mary, an' she knowin' the news you had for us, an' wouldn't let on; but it's all the more welcomer now, for we were on our last lap!

VOICE OF JOHNNY INSIDE. What are you kickin' up all the racket for?

BOYLE (*roughly*). I'm takin' off me moleskin trousers!

JOHNNY. Can't you do it, then, without lettin' th' whole house know you're takin' off your trousers? What d'ye want puttin' them on an' takin' them off again?

BOYLE. Will you let me alone, will you let me alone? Am I never goin' to be done thryin' to please th' whole o' yous?

MRS. BOYLE (*to* BENTHAM). You must excuse th' state o' th' place, Mr. Bentham; th' minute I turn me back that man o' mine always makes a litther o' th' place, a litther o' th' place.

BENTHAM. Don't worry, Mrs. Boyle; it's all right, I assure . . .

BOYLE (*inside*). Where's me braces; where in th' name o' God did I leave me braces. . . . Ay, did you see where I put me braces?

JOHNNY (*inside, calling out*). Ma, will you come in here an' take da away ou' o' this or he'll dhrive me mad.

MRS. BOYLE (*going towards door*). Dear, dear, dear, that man'll be lookin' for somethin'

38

on th' day o' Judgement. (*Looking into room
and calling to* BOYLE) Look at your braces, man,
hangin' round your neck!

BOYLE (*inside*). Aw, Holy God!

MRS. BOYLE (*calling*). Johnny, Johnny, come
out here for a minute.

JOHNNY. Ah, leave Johnny alone, an' don't
be annoyin' him!

MRS. BOYLE. Come on, Johnny, till I introduce you to Mr. Bentham. (*To* BENTHAM)
Me son, Mr. Bentham; he's afther goin'
through the mill. He was only a chiselur of
a Boy Scout in Easter Week, when he got hit
in the hip; and his arm was blew off in the
fight in O'Connell Street. (JOHNNY *comes in.*)
Here he is, Mr. Bentham; Mr. Bentham,
Johnny. None can deny he done his bit for
Irelan', if that's goin' to do him any good.

JOHNNY (*boastfully*). I'd do it agen, ma,
I'd do it agen; for a principle's a principle.

MRS. BOYLE. Ah, you lost your best principle, me boy, when you lost your arm; them's
the only sort o' principles that's any good to a
workin' man.

JOHNNY. Ireland only half free'll never be
at peace while she has a son left to pull a
trigger.

MRS. BOYLE. To be sure, to be sure—no

bread's a lot betther than half a loaf. (*Calling loudly into* BOYLE) Will you hurry up there?

> (BOYLE *enters in his best trousers, which aren't too good, and looks very uncomfortable in his collar and tie.*)

MRS. BOYLE. This is me husband; Mr. Boyle, Mr. Bentham.

BENTHAM. Ah, very glad to know you, Mr. Boyle. How are you?

BOYLE. Ah, I'm not too well at all; I suffer terrible with pains in me legs. Juno can tell you there what . . .

MRS. BOYLE. You won't have many pains in your legs when you hear what Mr. Bentham has to tell you.

BENTHAM. Juno! What an interesting name! It reminds one of Homer's glorious story of ancient gods and heroes.

BOYLE. Yis, doesn't it? You see, Juno was born an' christened in June; I met her in June; we were married in June, an' Johnny was born in June, so wan day I says to her, "You should ha' been called Juno," an' the name stuck to her ever since.

MRS. BOYLE. Here, we can talk o' them things agen; let Mr. Bentham say what he has to say now.

BENTHAM. Well, Mr. Boyle, I suppose

40

you'll remember a Mr. Ellison of Santry—
he's a relative of yours, I think.

BOYLE (*viciously*). Is it that prognosticator
an' procrastinator! Of course I remember
him.

BENTHAM. Well, he's dead, Mr. Boyle . . .

BOYLE. Sorra many'll go into mournin' for
him.

MRS. BOYLE. Wait till you hear what Mr.
Bentham has to say, an' then, maybe, you'll
change your opinion.

BENTHAM. A week before he died he sent
for me to write his will for him. He told me
that there were two only that he wished to
leave his property to: his second cousin,
Michael Finnegan of Santry, and John Boyle,
his first cousin of Dublin.

BOYLE (*excitedly*). Me, is it me, me?

BENTHAM. You, Mr. Boyle; I'll read a
copy of the will that I have here with me,
which has been duly filed in the Court of
Probate. (*He takes a paper from his pocket and
reads*):

6th February 1922.

This is the last Will and Testament of William
Ellison, of Santry, in the County of Dublin. I hereby
order and wish my property to be sold and divided as
follows:—

£20 to the St. Vincent De Paul Society.

£60 for Masses for the repose of my soul (5s. for Each Mass).

The rest of my property to be divided between my first and second cousins.

I hereby appoint Timothy Buckly, of Santry, and Hugh Brierly, of Coolock, to be my Executors.

(*Signed*)   WILLIAM ELLISON.
HUGH BRIERLY.
TIMOTHY BUCKLY.
CHARLES BENTHAM, N.T.

BOYLE (*eagerly*). An' how much'll be comin' out of it, Mr. Bentham?

BENTHAM. The Executors told me that half of the property would be anything between £1500 and £2000.

MARY. A fortune, father, a fortune!

JOHNNY. We'll be able to get out o' this place now, an' go somewhere we're not known.

MRS. BOYLE. You won't have to trouble about a job for awhile, Jack.

BOYLE (*fervently*). I'll never doubt the goodness o' God agen.

BENTHAM. I congratulate you, Mr. Boyle. (*They shake hands.*)

BOYLE. An' now, Mr. Bentham, you'll have to have a wet.

BENTHAM. A wet?

BOYLE. A wet—a jar—a boul!

42

MRS. BOYLE. Jack, you're speakin' to Mr. Bentham, an' not to Joxer.

BOYLE (*solemnly*). Juno . . . Mary . . . Johnny . . . we'll have to go into mournin' at wanst. . . . I never expected that poor Bill ud die so sudden. . . . Well, we all have to die some day . . . you, Juno, to-day . . . an' me, maybe, to-morrow. . . . It's sad, but it can't be helped. . . . Requiescat in pace . . . or, usin' our oul' tongue like St. Patrick or St. Briget, Guh sayeree jeea ayera!

MARY. Oh, father, that's not Rest in Peace; that's God save Ireland.

BOYLE. U-u-ugh, it's all the same—isn't it a prayer? . . . Juno, I'm done with Joxer; he's nothin' but a prognosticator an' a . . .

JOXER (*climbing angrily through the window and bounding into the room*). You're done with Joxer, are you? Maybe you thought I'd stop on the roof all the night for you! Joxer out on the roof with the win' blowin' through him was nothin' to you an' your friend with the collar an' tie!

MRS. BOYLE. What in the name o' God brought you out on the roof; what were you doin' there?

JOXER (*ironically*). I was dhreamin' I was standin' on the bridge of a ship, an' she sailin'

43

the Antartic Ocean, an' it blowed, an' blowed, an' I lookin' up at the sky an' sayin', what is the stars, what is the stars?

MRS. BOYLE (*opening the door and standing at it*). Here, get ou' o' this, Joxer Daly; I was always thinkin' you had a slate off.

JOXER (*moving to the door*). I have to laugh every time I look at the deep-sea sailor; an' a row on a river ud make him sea-sick!

BOYLE. Get ou' o' this before I take the law into me own hands!

JOXER (*going out*). Say aw rewaeawr, but not good-bye. Lookin' for work, an' prayin' to God he won't get it!   (*He goes.*)

MRS. BOYLE. I'm tired tellin' you what Joxer was; maybe now you see yourself the kind he is.

BOYLE. He'll never blow the froth off a pint o' mine agen, that's a sure thing. Johnny . . . Mary . . . you're to keep yourselves to yourselves for the future. Juno, I'm done with Joxer. . . . I'm a new man from this out. . . . (*Clasping* JUNO's *hand, and singing emotionally*):

Oh, me darlin' Juno, I will be thrue to thee;
Me own, me darlin' Juno, you're all the world to me.

CURTAIN

44

ACT II

SCENE: *The same, but the furniture is more plentiful, and of a vulgar nature. A glaringly upholstered arm-chair and lounge ; cheap pictures and photos everywhere. Every available spot is ornamented with huge vases filled with artificial flowers. Crossed festoons of coloured paper chains stretch from end to end of ceiling. On the table is an old attaché case. It is about six in the evening, and two days after the First Act.* BOYLE, *in his shirt sleeves, is voluptuously stretched on the sofa; he is smoking a clay pipe. He is half asleep. A lamp is lighting on the table. After a few moments' pause the voice of* JOXER *is heard singing softly outside at the door----"Me pipe I'll smoke, as I dhrive me moke—are you there, Mor . . . ee . . . ar . . . i . . . teee!"*

45

BOYLE (*leaping up, takes a pen in his hand and busies himself with papers*). Come along, Joxer, me son, come along.

JOXER (*putting his head in*). Are you be yourself?

BOYLE. Come on, come on; that doesn't matther; I'm masther now, an' I'm goin' to remain masther.

(JOXER *comes in.*)

JOXER. How d'ye feel now, as a man o' money?

BOYLE (*solemnly*). It's a responsibility, Joxer, a great responsibility.

JOXER. I suppose 'tis now, though you wouldn't think it.

BOYLE. Joxer, han' me over that attackey case on the table there. (JOXER *hands the case.*) Ever since the Will was passed I've run hundhreds o' dockyments through me hans— I tell you, you have to keep your wits about you. (*He busies himself with papers.*)

JOXER. Well, I won't disturb you; I'll dhrop in when . . .

BOYLE (*hastily*). It's all right, Joxer, this is the last one to be signed to-day. (*He signs a paper, puts it into the case, which he shuts with a snap, and sits back pompously in the chair.*) Now, Joxer, you want to see me; I'm at

46

your service—what can I do for you, me man?

JOXER. I've just dhropped in with the £3 : 5s. that Mrs. Madigan riz on the blankets an' table for you, an' she says you're to be in no hurry payin' it back.

BOYLE. She won't be long without it; I expect the first cheque for a couple o' hundhred any day. There's the five bob for yourself— go on, take it, man; it'll not be the last you'll get from the Captain. Now an' agen we have our differ, but we're there together all the time.

JOXER. Me for you, an' you for me, like the two Musketeers.

BOYLE. Father Farrell stopped me to-day an' tole me how glad he was I fell in for the money.

JOXER. He'll be stoppin' you ofen enough now; I suppose it was " Mr. " Boyle with him?

BOYLE. He shuk me be the han'. . . .

JOXER (*ironically*). I met with Napper Tandy, an' he shuk me be the han'!

BOYLE. You're seldom asthray, Joxer, but you're wrong shipped this time. What you're sayin' of Father Farrell is very near to blasfeemey. I don't like any one to talk disrespectful of Father Farrell.

47

JOXER. You're takin' me up wrong, Captain; I wouldn't let a word be said agen Father Farrell—the heart o' the rowl, that's what he is; I always said he was a darlin' man, a daarlin' man.

BOYLE. Comin' up the stairs who did I meet but that bummer, Nugent. " I seen you talkin' to Father Farrell," says he, with a grin on him. " He'll be folleyin' you," says he, " like a Guardian Angel from this out "—all the time the oul' grin on him, Joxer.

JOXER. I never seen him yet but he had that oul' grin on him!

BOYLE. " Mr. Nugent," says I, " Father Farrell is a man o' the people, an', as far as I know the History o' me country, the priests was always in the van of the fight for Irelan's freedom."

JOXER (*fervently*):

Who was it led the van, Soggart Aroon?
Since the fight first began, Soggart Aroon?

BOYLE. " Who are you tellin'," says he? " Didn't they let down the Fenians, an' didn't they do in Parnell? An' now . . ." " You ought to be ashamed o' yourself," says I, interruptin' him, " not to know the History o' your country." An' I left him gawkin' where he was.

JOXER. Where ignorance 's bliss 'tis folly to be wise; I wondher did he ever read the Story o' Irelan'.

BOYLE. Be J. L. Sullivan? Don't you know he didn't.

JOXER. Ah, it's a darlin' buk, a daarlin' buk!

BOYLE. You'd betther be goin', now, Joxer, his Majesty, Bentham, 'll be here any minute, now.

JOXER. Be the way things is lookin', it'll be a match between him an' Mary. She's thrun over Jerry altogether. Well, I hope it will, for he's a darlin' man.

BOYLE. I'm glad you think so—I don't. (*Irritably*) What's darlin' about him?

JOXER (*nonplussed*). I only seen him twiced; if you want to know me, come an' live with me.

BOYLE. He's too ignified for me—to hear him talk you'd think he knew as much as a Boney's Oraculum. He's given up his job as teacher, an' is goin' to become a solicitor in Dublin—he's been studyin' law. I suppose he thinks I'll set him up, but he's wrong shipped. An' th' other fella—Jerry's as bad. The two o' them ud give you a pain in your face, listenin' to them; Jerry believin' in nothin', an' Bentham believin' in everythin'.

One that says all is God an' no man; an'
th' other that says all is man an' no God!

JOXER. Well, I'll be off now.

BOYLE. Don't forget to dhrop down afther
awhile; we'll have a quiet jar, an' a song or
two.

JOXER. Never fear.

BOYLE. An' tell Mrs. Madigan that I hope
we'll have the pleasure of her organization at
our little enthertainment.

JOXER. Righto; we'll come down together.
(*He goes out.*)

(JOHNNY *comes from room on left, and sits
down moodily at the fire.* BOYLE *looks
at him for a few moments, and shakes
his head. He fills his pipe.*)

VOICE OF JUNO AT THE DOOR. Open the
door, Jack; this thing has me nearly kilt with
the weight.

(BOYLE *opens the door.* JUNO *enters
carrying the box of a gramophone,
followed by* MARY *carrying the horn
and some parcels.* JUNO *leaves the
box on the table and flops into a chair.*)

JUNO. Carryin' that from Henry Street was
no joke.

BOYLE. U-u-ugh, that's a grand-lookin'
insthrument—how much was it?

JUNO. Pound down, an' five to be paid at two shillins a week.

BOYLE. That's reasonable enough.

JUNO. I'm afraid we're runnin' into too much debt; first the furniture, an' now this.

BOYLE. The whole lot won't be much out of £2000.

MARY. I don't know what you wanted a gramophone for—I know Charlie hates them; he says they're destructive of real music.

BOYLE. Desthructive of music—that fella ud give you a pain in your face. All a gramophone wants is to be properly played; it's thrue wondher is only felt when everythins quiet—what a gramophone wants is dead silence!

MARY. But, father, Jerry says the same; afther all you can only appreciate music when your ear is properly trained.

BOYLE. That's another fella ud give you a pain in your face. Properly thrained! I suppose you couldn't appreciate football unless your fut was properly thrained.

MRS. BOYLE (to MARY). Go on in ower that an' dress, or Charlie 'll be in on you, an' tea nor nothin 'll be ready.

(MARY goes into room left.)

51

MRS. BOYLE (*arranging table for tea*). You didn't look at our new gramophone, Johnny?

JOHNNY. 'Tisn't gramophones I'm thinking of.

MRS. BOYLE. An' what is it you're thinkin' of, allanna?

JOHNNY. Nothin', nothin', nothin'.

MRS. BOYLE. Sure, you must be thinkin' of somethin'; it's yourself that has yourself the way y'are; sleepin' wan night in me sisther's, an' the nex' in your father's brother's—you'll get no rest goin' on that way.

JOHNNY. I can rest nowhere, nowhere, nowhere.

MRS. BOYLE. Sure, you're not thryin' to rest anywhere.

JOHNNY. Let me alone, let me alone, let me alone, for God's sake.

(*A knock at street door.*)

MRS. BOYLE (*in a flutter*). Here he is; here's Mr. Bentham!

BOYLE. Well, there's room for him; it's a pity there's not a brass band to play him in.

MRS. BOYLE. We'll han' the tea round, an' not be clusthered round the table, as if we never seen nothin'.

(*Steps are heard approaching, and* JUNO,

52

opening the door, allows BENTHAM *to enter.*)

JUNO. Give your hat an' stick to Jack, there . . . sit down, Mr. Bentham . . . no, not there . . . in th' easy chair be the fire . . . there, that's bether.   Mary'll be out to you in a minute.

BOYLE (*solemnly*). I seen be the paper this mornin' that Consols was down half per cent. That's serious, min' you, an' shows the whole counthry's in a state o' chassis.

MRS. BOYLE. What's Consols, Jack?

BOYLE. Consols?   Oh, Consols is—oh, there's no use tellin' women what Consols is —th' wouldn't undherstand.

BENTHAM. It's just as you were saying, Mr. Boyle . . .

(MARY *enters, charmingly dressed.*)

BENTHAM. Oh, good evening, Mary; how pretty you're looking!

MARY (*archly*). Am I?

BOYLE. We were just talkin' when you kem in, Mary; I was tellin' Mr. Bentham that the whole counthry's in a state o' chassis.

MARY (*to* BENTHAM). Would you prefer the green or the blue ribbon round me hair, Charlie?

MRS. BOYLE. Mary, your father's speakin'.

BOYLE (*rapidly*). I was jus' tellin' Mr.
Bentham that the whole counthry's in a state o'
chassis.

MARY. I'm sure you're frettin', da, whether
it is or no.

MRS. BOYLE. With all our churches an'
religions, the worl's not a bit the betther.

BOYLE (*with a commanding gesture*). Tay!

(MARY *and* MRS. BOYLE *dispense the tea.*)

MRS. BOYLE. An' Irelan's takin' a leaf out
o' the worl's buk; when we got the makin' of
our own laws I thought we'd never stop to look
behind us, but instead of that we never stopped
to look before us!   If the people ud folley up
their religion betther there'd be a betther
chance for us—what do you think, Mr.
Bentham?

BENTHAM. I'm afraid I can't venture to
express an opinion on that point, Mrs. Boyle;
dogma has no attraction for me.

MRS. BOYLE. I forgot you didn't hold with
us: what's this you said you were?

BENTHAM. A Theosophist, Mrs. Boyle.

MRS. BOYLE. An' what in the name o' God 's
a Theosophist?

BOYLE. A Theosophist, Juno, 's a—tell her,
Mr. Bentham, tell her.

BENTHAM. It's hard to explain in a few

words: Theosophy's founded on The Vedas, the religious books of the East. It's central theme is the existence of an all-pervading Spirit —the Life-Breath. Nothing really exists but this one Universal Life Breath. And whatever even seems to exist separately from this Life-Breath, doesn't really exist at all. It is all vital force in man, in all animals, and in all vegetation. This Life-Breath is called the Prawna.

MRS. BOYLE. The Prawna! What a comical name!

BOYLE. Prawna; yis, the Prawna. (*Blowing gently through his lips*) That's the Prawna!

MRS. BOYLE. Whist, whist, Jack.

BENTHAM. The happiness of man depends upon his sympathy with this Spirit. Men who have reached a high state of excellence are called Yogi. Some men become Yogi in a short time, it may take others millions of years.

BOYLE. Yogi! I seen hundhreds of them in the streets o' San Francisco.

BENTHAM. It is said by these Yogi that if we practise certain mental exercises that we would have powers denied to others—for instance, the faculty of seeing things that happen miles and miles away.

MRS. BOYLE. I wouldn't care to meddle with

that sort o' belief; it's a very curious religion, altogether.

BOYLE. What's curious about it? Isn't all religions curious; if they weren't, you wouldn't get any one to believe them. But religions is passin' away—they've had their day like everything else. Take the real Dublin people, f'rinstance: they know more about Charlie Chaplin an' Tommy Mix than they do about SS. Peter an' Paul!

MRS. BOYLE. You don't believe in ghosts, Mr. Bentham?

MARY. Don't you know he doesn't, mother?

BENTHAM. I don't know that, Mary. Scientists are beginning to think that what we call ghosts are sometimes seen by persons of a certain nature. They say that sensational actions, such as the killing of a person, demands great energy, and that that energy lingers in the place where the action occurred. People may live in the place and see nothing, when some one may come along whose personality has some peculiar connection with the energy of the place, and, in a flash, the person sees the whole affair.

JOHNNY (*rising swiftly, pale and affected*). What sort o' talk is this to be goin' on with? Is there nothin' bether to be talkin' about but

the killin' o' people? My God, isn't it bad
enough for these things to happen without
talkin' about them! (*He hurriedly goes into the
room on left.*)

BENTHAM. Oh, I'm very sorry, Mrs. Boyle;
I never thought . . .

MRS. BOYLE (*apologetically*). Never mind, Mr.
Bentham, he's very touchy. (*A frightened
scream is heard from* JOHNNY *inside.*)

MRS. BOYLE. Mother of God, what's that?

> (*He rushes out again, his face pale, his
> lips twitching, his limbs trembling.*)

JOHNNY. Shut the door, shut the door,
quick, for God's sake! Great God, have mercy
on me! Blessed Mother o' God, shelter me,
shelther your son!

MRS. BOYLE (*catching him in her arms*). What's
wrong with you? What ails you? Sit down,
sit down, here, on the bed . . . there now
. . . there now.

MARY. Johnny, Johnny, what ails you?

JOHNNY. I seen him, I seen him . . .
kneelin' in front o' the statue . . . merciful
Jesus, have pity on me!

MRS. BOYLE (*to* BOYLE). Get him a glass o'
whisky . . . quick, man, an' don't stand
gawkin'.

> (BOYLE *gets the whisky.*)

57

JOHNNY. Sit here, sit here, mother . . . between me an' the door.

MRS. BOYLE. I'll sit beside you as long as you like, only tell me what was it came across you at all?

JOHNNY (*after taking some drink*). I seen him. . . . I seen Robbie Tancred kneelin' down before the statue . . . an' the red light shinin' on him . . . an' when I went in . . . he turned an' looked at me . . . an' I seen the wouns bleedin' in his breast. . . . Oh, why did he look at me like that . . . it wasn't my fault that he was done in. . . . Mother o' God, keep him away from me!

MRS. BOYLE. There, there, child, you've imagined it all. There was nothin' there at all—it was the red light you seen, an' the talk we had put all the rest into your head. Here, dhrink more o' this—it'll do you good. . . . An', now, stretch yourself down on the bed for a little. (*To* BOYLE) Go in, Jack, an' show him it was only in his own head it was.

BOYLE (*making no move*). E-e-e-e-eh; it's all nonsense; it was only a shadda he saw.

MARY. Mother o' God, he made me heart lep!

BENTHAM. It was simply due to an over-wrought imagination—we all get that way at times.

58

MRS. BOYLE. There, dear, lie down in the bed, an' I'll put the quilt across you . . . e-e-e-eh, that's it . . . you'll be as right as the mail in a few minutes.

JOHNNY. Mother, go into the room an' see if the light's lightin' before the statue.

MRS. BOYLE (*to* BOYLE). Jack, run in an' see if the light's lightin' before the statue.

BOYLE (*to* MARY). Mary, slip in an' see if the light's lightin' before the statue.

(MARY *hesitates to go in*.)

BENTHAM. It's all right; Mary, I'll go.

(*He goes into the room; remains for a few moments, and returns*.)

BENTHAM. Everything's just as it was—the light burning bravely before the statue.

BOYLE. Of course ; I knew it was all nonsense.

(*A knock at the door*.)

BOYLE (*going to open the door*). E-e-e-e-eh.

(*He opens it, and* JOXER, *followed by* MRS. MADIGAN, *enters*. MRS. MADIGAN *is a strong, dapper little woman of about forty-five; her face is almost always a widespread smile of complacency. She is a woman who, in manner at least, can mourn with them that mourn, and rejoice with them that do rejoice. When*

59

*she is feeling comfortable, she is inclined
to be reminiscent; when others say anything, or following a statement made by
herself, she has a habit of putting her
head a little to one side, and nodding
it rapidly several times in succession,
like a bird pecking at a hard berry.
Indeed, she has a good deal of the bird
in her, but the bird instinct is by no
means a melodious one. She is
ignorant, vulgar and forward, but her
heart is generous withal. For instance,
she would help a neighbour's sick child;
she would probably kill the child, but
her intentions would be to cure it; she
would be more at home helping a dray-
man to lift a fallen horse. She is
dressed in a rather soiled grey dress
and a vivid purple blouse; in her hair
is a huge comb, ornamented with huge
coloured beads. She enters with a
gliding step, beaming smile and nodding
head.* BOYLE *receives them effusively.*)

BOYLE. Come on in, Mrs. Madigan; come
on in; I was afraid you weren't comin'. . . .
(*Slyly*) There's some people able to dhress, ay,
Joxer?

JOXER. Fair as the blossoms that bloom in

the May, an' sweet as the scent of the new-mown hay. . . . Ah, well she may wear them.

MRS. MADIGAN (*looking at* MARY). I know some as are as sweet as the blossoms that bloom in the May—oh, no names, no pack dhrill!

BOYLE. An', now, I'll inthroduce the pair o' yous to Mary's intended: Mr. Bentham, this is Mrs. Madigan, an oul' back-parlour neighbour, that, if she could help it at all, ud never see a body shuk!

BENTHAM (*rising, and tentatively shaking the hand of* MRS. MADIGAN). I'm sure, it's a great pleasure to know you, Mrs. Madigan.

MRS. MADIGAN. An' I'm goin' to tell you, Mr. Bentham, you're goin' to get as nice a bit o' skirt in Mary, there, as ever you seen in your puff. Not like some of the dhressed-up dolls that's knockin' about lookin' for men when it's a skelpin' they want. I remember, as well as I remember yesterday, the day she was born—of a Tuesday, the 25th o' June, in the year 1901, at thirty-three minutes past wan in the day be Foley's clock, the pub at the corner o' the street. A cowld day it was too, for the season o' the year, an' I remember sayin' to Joxer, there, who I met comin' up th' stairs, that the new arrival in Boyle's ud grow up a hardy chiselur if it lived, an that she'd be somethin' one o' these days that nobody suspected, an' so signs on it, here she is to-day, goin' to be married to a young man lookin' as if he'd be fit to commensurate in any position in life it ud please God to call him!

BOYLE (*effusively*). Sit down, Mrs. Madigan, sit down, me oul' sport. (*To* BENTHAM) This is Joxer Daly, Past Chief Ranger of the Dear Little Shamrock Branch of the Irish National Foresters, an oul' front-top neighbour, that never despaired, even in the darkest days of Ireland's sorra.

JOXER. Nil desperandum, Captain, nil desperandum.

BOYLE. Sit down, Joxer, sit down. The two of us was ofen in a tight corner.

MRS. BOYLE. Ay, in Foley's snug!

JOXER. An' we kem out of it flyin', we kem out of it flyin', Captain.

BOYLE. An', now, for a dhrink—I know yous won't refuse an oul' friend.

MRS. MADIGAN (*to* JUNO). Is Johnny not well, Mrs. . . .

MRS. BOYLE (*warningly*). S-s-s-sh.

MRS. MADIGAN. Oh, the poor darlin'.

BOYLE. Well, Mrs. Madigan, is it tea or what?

MRS. MADIGAN. Well, speakin' for meself, I jus' had me tea a minute ago, an' I'm afraid to dhrink any more—I'm never the same when I dhrink too much tay. Thanks, all the same, Mr. Boyle.

BOYLE. Well, what about a bottle o' stout or a dhrop o' whisky?

MRS. MADIGAN. A bottle o' stout ud be a little too heavy for me stummock afther me tay. . . . A-a-ah, I'll thry the ball o' malt.

(BOYLE *prepares the whisky*.)

MRS. MADIGAN. There's nothin' like a ball o' malt occasional like—too much of it isn't good. (*To* BOYLE, *who is adding water*) Ah, God, Johnny, don't put too much wather on it! (*She drinks*.) I suppose yous'll be lavin' this place.

BOYLE. I'm looking for a place near the sea; I'd like the place that you might say was me cradle, to be me grave as well. The sea is always callin' me.

JOXER. She is callin', callin', callin', in the win' an' on the sea.

BOYLE. Another dhrop o' whisky, Mrs. Madigan?

MRS. MADIGAN. Well, now, it ud be hard to refuse seein' the suspicious times that's in it.

BOYLE (*with a commanding gesture*). Song! . . . Juno . . . Mary . . . " Home to Our Mountins "!

MRS. MADIGAN (*enthusiastically*). Hear, hear!

JOXER. Oh, tha's a darlin' song, a daarlin' song!

MARY (*bashfully*). Ah no, da; I'm not in a singin' humour.

MRS. MADIGAN. Gawn with you, child, an' you only goin' to be marrid; I remember as well as I remember yesterday,—it was on a lovely August evenin', exactly, accordin' to date, fifteen years ago, come the Tuesday folleyin' the nex' that's comin' on, when me own man (*the Lord be good to him*) an' me was sittin' shy together in a doty little nook on a counthry road, adjacent to The Stiles. " That'll scratch your lovely, little white neck," says he, ketchin' hould of a danglin' bramble branch, holdin' clusters of the loveliest flowers you ever seen, an' breakin' it off, so that his arm fell, accidental like, roun' me waist, an' as I felt it tightenin', an' tightenin', an' tightenin', I thought me buzzum was every minute goin' to burst out into a roystherin' song about

The little green leaves that were shakin' on the
    threes,
The gallivantin' buttherflies, an' buzzin' o' the bees!

BOYLE. Ordher for the song!

JUNO. Come on, Mary—we'll do our best.

(JUNO *and* MARY *stand up, and choosing a suitable position, sing simply "Home to Our Mountains".*)

(*They bow to company, and return to their places.*)

BOYLE (*emotionally, at the end of song*). Lull . . . me . . . to . . . rest!

JOXER (*clapping his hands*). Bravo, bravo! Darlin' girulls, darlin' girulls!

MRS. MADIGAN. Juno, I never seen you in betther form.

BENTHAM. Very nicely rendered indeed.

MRS. MADIGAN. A noble call, a noble call!

MRS. BOYLE. What about yourself, Mrs. Madigan?

(*After some coaxing,* MRS. MADIGAN *rises, and in a quavering voice sings the following verse*):

If I were a blackbird I'd whistle and sing;
I'd follow the ship that my thrue love was in;
An' on the top riggin', I'd there build me nest,
An' at night I would sleep on me Willie's white breast!

(*Becoming husky, amid applause, she sits down.*)

MRS. MADIGAN. Ah, me voice is too husky

now, Juno; though I remember the time when
Maisie Madigan could sing like a nightingale
at matin' time. I remember as well as I
remember yestherday, at a party given to
celebrate the comin' of the first chiselur to
Annie an' Benny Jimeson—who was the barber,
yous may remember, in Henrietta Street, that,
afther Easter Week, hung out a green, white
an' orange pole, an', then, when the Tans
started their Jazz dancin', whipped it in agen,
an' stuck out a red, white an' blue wan instead,
givin' as an excuse that a barber's pole was
strictly non-political — singin' " An' You'll
Remember Me ", with the top notes quiverin'
in a dead hush of pethrified attention, folleyed
be a clappin' o' hans that shuk the tumblers on
the table, an' capped be Jimeson, the barber,
sayin' that it was the best rendherin' of " You'll
Remember Me " he ever heard in his natural!

BOYLE (*peremptorily*). Ordher for Joxer's
song!

JOXER. Ah no, I couldn't; don't ass me,
Captain.

BOYLE. Joxer's song, Joxer's song—give us
wan of your shut-eyed wans. (JOXER *settles
himself in his chair; takes a drink; clears his
throat; solemnly closes his eyes, and begins to sing
in a very querulous voice*):

66

She is far from the lan' where her young hero sleeps,
An' lovers around her are sighing   (*He hesitates.*)
An' lovers around her are sighin' . . . sighin' . . .
    sighin' . . .   (*A pause.*)

BOYLE (*imitating* JOXER):

And lovers around her are sighing!

What's the use of you thryin' to sing the song
if you don't know it?

MARY. Thry another one, Mr. Daly—
maybe you'd be more fortunate.

MRS. MADIGAN. Gawn, Joxer; thry another
wan.

JOXER (*starting again*):

I have heard the mavis singin' his love song to the morn;
I have seen the dew-dhrop clingin' to the rose jus'
    newly born; but . . . but . . . (*frantically*)
    To the rose jus' newly born . . . newly born
    . . . born.

JOHNNY. Mother, put on the gramophone,
for God's sake, an' stop Joxer's bawlin'.

BOYLE (*commandingly*).   Gramophone! . . .
I hate to see fellas thryin' to do what they're
not able to do.

> (BOYLE *arranges the gramophone, and is
> about to start it, when voices are heard
> of persons descending the stairs.*)

67

MRS. BOYLE (*warningly*). Whisht, Jack, don't put it on, don't put it on yet; this must be poor Mrs. Tancred comin' down to go to the hospital—I forgot all about them bringin' the body to the church to-night.   Open the door, Mary, an' give them a bit o' light.

> (MARY *opens the door, and* MRS. TANCRED *—a very old woman, obviously shaken by the death of her son—appears, accompanied by several neighbours. The first few phrases are spoken before they appear.*)

FIRST NEIGHBOUR. It's a sad journey we're goin' on, but God's good, an' the Republicans won't be always down.

MRS. TANCRED. Ah, what good is that to me now?   Whether they're up or down—it won't bring me darlin' boy from the grave.

MRS. BOYLE. Come in an' have a hot cup o' tay, Mrs. Tancred, before you go.

MRS. TANCRED. Ah, I can take nothin' now, Mrs. Boyle—I won't be long afther him.

FIRST NEIGHBOUR. Still an' all, he died a noble death, an' we'll bury him like a king.

MRS. TANCRED. An' I'll go on livin' like a pauper.   Ah, what's the pains I suffered bringin' him into the world to carry him to his cradle, to the pains I'm sufferin' now, carryin' him out o' the world to bring him to his grave!

MARY. It would be better for you not to go at all, Mrs. Tancred, but to stay at home beside the fire with some o' the neighbours.

MRS. TANCRED. I seen the first of him, an' I'll see the last of him.

MRS. BOYLE. You'd want a shawl, Mrs. Tancred; it's a cowld night, an' the win's blowin' sharp.

MRS. MADIGAN (*rushing out*). I've a shawl above.

MRS. TANCRED. Me home is gone, now; he was me only child, an' to think that he was lyin' for a whole night stretched out on the side of a lonely counthry lane, with his head, his darlin' head, that I ofen kissed an' fondled, half hidden in the wather of a runnin' brook. An' I'm told he was the leadher of the ambush where me nex' door neighbour, Mrs. Mannin', lost her Free State soldier son. An' now here's the two of us oul' women, standin' one on each side of a scales o' sorra, balanced be the bodies of our two dead darlin' sons. (MRS. MADIGAN *returns, and wraps a shawl around her.*) God bless you, Mrs. Madigan. . . . (*She moves slowly towards the door*) Mother o' God, Mother o' God, have pity on the pair of us! . . .

O Blessed Virgin, where were you when me darlin' son was riddled with bullets, when me darlin' son was riddled with bullets! . . . Sacred Heart of the Crucified Jesus, take away our hearts o' stone . . . an' give us hearts o' flesh! . . . Take away this murdherin' hate . . . an' give us Thine own eternal love!

(*They pass out of the room.*)

MRS. BOYLE (*explanatorily to* BENTHAM). That was Mrs. Tancred of the two-pair back; her son was found, e'er yestherday, lyin' out beyant Finglas riddled with bullets. A Die-hard he was, be all accounts. He was a nice quiet boy, but lattherly he went to hell, with his Republic first, an' Republic last an' Republic over all. He ofen took tea with us here, in the oul' days, an' Johnny, there, an' him used to be always together.

JOHNNY. Am I always to be havin' to tell you that he was no friend o' mine; I never cared for him, an' he could never stick me. It's not because he was Commandant of the Battalion that I was Quarther-Masther of, that we were friends.

MRS. BOYLE. He's gone now—the Lord be good to him! God help his poor oul' creature of a mother, for no matther whose friend or enemy he was, he was her poor son.

BENTHAM. The whole thing is terrible, Mrs. Boyle; but the only way to deal with a mad dog is to destroy him.

MRS. BOYLE. An' to think of me forgettin' about him bein' brought to the church to-night, an' we singin' an' all, but it was well we hadn't the gramophone goin', anyhow.

BOYLE. Even if we had aself. We've nothin' to do with these things, one way or t'other. That's the Government's business, an' let them do what we're payin' them for doin'.

MRS. BOYLE. I'd like to know how a body's not to mind these things; look at the way they're afther leavin' the people in this very house. Hasn't the whole house, nearly, been massacreed? There's young Dougherty's husband with his leg off; Mrs. Travers that had her son blew up be a mine in Inchegeela, in Co. Cork; Mrs. Mannin' that lost wan of her sons in an ambush a few weeks ago, an' now, poor Mrs. Tancred's only child gone West with his body made a collandher of. Sure, if it's not our business, I don't know whose business it is.

BOYLE. Here, there, that's enough about them things; they don't affect us, an' we needn't give a damn. If they want a wake, well, let them have a wake. When I was a sailor, I was always resigned to meet with a wathery grave; an', if they want to be soldiers, well, there's no use o' them squealin' when they meet a soldier's fate.

JOXER. Let me like a soldier fall—me breast expandin' to th' ball!

MRS. BOYLE. In wan way, she deserves all she got; for lately, she let th' Die-hards make an open house of th' place; an' for th' last couple of months, either when th' sun was risin', or when th' sun was settin', you had C.I.D. men burstin' into your room, assin' you where were you born, where were you christened, where were you married, an' where would you be buried!

JOHNNY. For God's sake, let us have no more o' this talk.

MRS. MADIGAN. What about Mr. Boyle's song before we start th' gramophone?

MARY (*getting her hat, and putting it on*). Mother, Charlie and I are goin' out for a little sthroll.

MRS. BOYLE. All right, darlin'.

BENTHAM (*going out with* MARY). We won't be long away, Mrs. Boyle.

MRS. MADIGAN. Gwan, Captain, gwan.

BOYLE. E-e-e-e-eh, I'd want to have a few

more jars in me, before I'd be in fettle for singin'.

JOXER. Give us that poem you writ t'other day. (*To the rest*) Aw, it's a darlin' poem, a daarlin' poem.

MRS. BOYLE. God bless us, is he startin' to write poetry!

BOYLE (*rising to his feet*). E-e-e-e-eh. (*He recites in an emotional, consequential manner the following verses*):

Shawn an' I were friends, sir, to me he was all in all.
His work was very heavy and his wages were very small.
None betther on th' beach as Docker, I'll go bail,
'Tis now I'm feelin' lonely, for to-day he lies in jail.
He was not what some call pious—seldom at church or
     prayer;
For the greatest scoundrels I know, sir, goes every
     Sunday there.
Fond of his pint—well, rather, but hated the Boss by
     creed
But never refused a copper to comfort a pal in need.

E-e-e-e-eh.   (*He sits down.*)

MRS. MADIGAN. Grand, grand; you should folly that up, you should folly that up.

JOXER. It's a daarlin' poem!

BOYLE (*delightedly*). E-e-e-e-eh.

JOHNNY. Are yous goin' to put on th' gramophone to-night, or are yous not?

MRS. BOYLE. Gwan, Jack, put on a record.

MRS. MADIGAN. Gwan, Captain, gwan.

BOYLE. Well, yous'll want to keep a dead silence.

(*He sets a record, starts the machine, and it begins to play " If you're Irish, come into the Parlour." As the tune is in full blare, the door is suddenly opened by a brisk, little bald-headed man, dressed circumspectly in a black suit; he glares fiercely at all in the room; he is "* NEEDLE NUGENT *", a tailor. He carries his hat in his hand.*)

NUGENT (*loudly, above the noise of the gramophone*). Are yous goin' to have that thing bawlin' an' the funeral of Mrs. Tancred's son passin' the house? Have none of yous any respect for the Irish people's National regard for the dead?

(BOYLE *stops the gramophone.*)

MRS. BOYLE. Maybe, Needle Nugent, it's nearly time we had a little less respect for the dead, an' a little more regard for the livin'.

MRS. MADIGAN. We don't want you, Mr. Nugent, to teach us what we learned at our mother's knee. You don't look yourself as if you were dyin' of grief; if y'ass Maisie Madigan anything, I'd call you a real thrue Die-hard an'

74

live-soft Republican, attendin' Republican
funerals in the day, an' stoppin' up half the
night makin' suits for the Civic Guards!

> (*Persons are heard running down to the
> street, some saying, "Here it is, here it
> is."* NUGENT *withdraws, and the rest,
> except* JOHNNY, *go to the window look-
> ing into the street, and look out. Sounds
> of a crowd coming nearer are heard;
> portion are singing*):

> To Jesus' Heart all burning
> With fervent love for men,
> My heart with fondest yearning
> Shall raise its joyful strain.
> While ages course along,
> Blest be with loudest song,
> The Sacred Heart of Jesus
> By every heart and tongue.

MRS. BOYLE. Here's the hearse, here's the
hearse!

BOYLE. There's t'oul' mother walkin' behin'
the coffin.

MRS. MADIGAN. You can hardly see the
coffin with the wreaths.

JOXER. Oh, it's a darlin' funeral, a daarlin'
funeral!

MRS. MADIGAN. We'd have a betther view
from the street.

BOYLE. Yes—this place ud give you a crick in your neck.

(*They leave the room, and go down.* JOHNNY *sits moodily by the fire.*)

(*A young man enters; he looks at* JOHNNY *for a moment.*)

THE YOUNG MAN. Quarther-Masther Boyle.

JOHNNY (*with a start*). The Mobilizer!

THE YOUNG MAN. You're not at the funeral?

JOHNNY. I'm not well.

THE YOUNG MAN. I'm glad I've found you; you were stoppin' at your aunt's; I called there but you'd gone. I've to give you an ordher to attend a Battalion Staff meetin' the night afther to-morrow.

JOHNNY. Where?

THE YOUNG MAN. I don't know; you're to meet me at the Pillar at eight o'clock; then we're to go to a place I'll be told of to-night; there we'll meet a mothor that'll bring us to the meeting. They think you might be able to know somethin' about them that gave the bend where Commandant Tancred was shelterin'.

JOHNNY. I'm not goin', then. I know nothing about Tancred.

THE YOUNG MAN (*at the door*). You'd bethher come for your own sake—remember your oath.

JOHNNY (*passionately*). I won't go! Haven't I done enough for Ireland! I've lost me arm, an' me hip's desthroyed so that I'll never be able to walk right agen! Good God, haven't I done enough for Ireland?

THE YOUNG MAN. Boyle, no man can do enough for Ireland!   (*He goes.*)
      (*Faintly in the distance the crowd is heard saying*):

Hail, Mary, full of grace, the Lord is with Thee;
Blessed art Thou amongst women, and blessed, etc.

CURTAIN

ACT III

SCENE: *The same as Act II. It is about half-past six on a November evening; a bright fire is burning in the grate;* MARY, *dressed to go out, is sitting on a chair by the fire, leaning forward, her hands under her chin, her elbows on her knees. A look of dejection, mingled with uncertain anxiety, is on her face. A lamp, turned low, is lighting on the table. The votive light under the picture of the Virgin gleams more redly than ever.* MRS. BOYLE *is putting on her hat and coat. It is two months later.*

MRS. BOYLE. An' has Bentham never even written to you since——not one line for the past month?

MARY (*tonelessly*). Not even a line, mother.

MRS. BOYLE. That's very curious. . . . What came between the two of yous at all? To leave you so sudden, an' yous so great together.

. . . To go away t' England, an' not to even leave you his address. . . . The way he was always bringin' you to dances, I thought he was mad afther you. Are you sure you said nothin' to him?

MARY. No, mother—at least nothing that could possibly explain his givin' me up.

MRS. BOYLE. You know you're a bit hasty at times, Mary, an' say things you shouldn't say.

MARY. I never said to him what I shouldn't say, I'm sure of that.

MRS. BOYLE. How are you sure of it?

MARY. Because I love him with all my heart and soul, mother. Why, I don't know; I often thought to myself that he wasn't the man poor Jerry was, but I couldn't help loving him, all the same.

MRS. BOYLE. But you shouldn't be frettin' the way you are; when a woman loses a man, she never knows what she's afther losin', to be sure, but, then, she never knows what she's afther gainin', either. You're not the one girl of a month ago—you look like one pinin' away. It's long ago I had a right to bring you to the doctor, instead of waitin' till to-night.

MARY. There's no necessity, really, mother, to go to the doctor; nothing serious is wrong

79

with me——I'm run down and disappointed, that's all.

MRS. BOYLE. I'll not wait another minute; I don't like the look of you at all. . . . I'm afraid we made a mistake in throwin' over poor Jerry. . . . He'd have been betther for you than that Bentham.

MARY. Mother, the best man for a woman is the one for whom she has the most love, and Charlie had it all.

MRS. BOYLE. Well, there's one thing to be said for him——he couldn't have been thinkin' of the money, or he wouldn't ha' left you . . . it must ha' been somethin' else.

MARY (*wearily*). I don't know . . . I don't know, mother . . . only I think . . .

MRS. BOYLE. What d'ye think?

MARY. I imagine . . . he thought . . . we weren't . . . good enough for him.

MRS. BOYLE. An' what was he himself, only a school teacher? Though I don't blame him for fightin' shy of people like that Joxer fella an' that oul' Madigan wan——nice sort o' people for your father to inthroduce to a man like Mr. Bentham. You might have told me all about this before now, Mary; I don't know why you like to hide everything from your mother; you knew Bentham, an' I'd ha' known

nothin' about it if it hadn't bin for the Will;
an' it was only to-day, afther long coaxin', that
you let out that he'd left you.

MARY. It would have been useless to tell
you—you wouldn't understand.

MRS. BOYLE (*hurt*). Maybe not. . . . Maybe
I wouldn't understand. . . . Well, we'll be
off now.

> (*She goes over to door left, and speaks to*
> BOYLE *inside*.)

MRS. BOYLE. We're goin' now to the doctor's.
Are you goin' to get up this evenin'?

BOYLE (*from inside*). The pains in me legs
is terrible! It's me should be poppin' off to
the doctor instead o' Mary, the way I feel.

MRS. BOYLE. Sorra mend you! A nice way
you were in last night—carried in in a frog's
march, dead to the world. If that's the way
you'll go on when you get the money it'll be
the grave for you, an asylum for me and the
Poorhouse for Johnny.

BOYLE. I thought you were goin'?

MRS. BOYLE. That's what has you as you
are—you can't bear to be spoken to. Knowin'
the way we are, up to our ears in debt, it's a
wondher you wouldn't ha' got up to go to th'
solicitor's an' see if we could ha' gotten a little
o' the money even.

BOYLE (*shouting*). I can't be goin' up there night, noon an' mornin', can I? He can't give the money till he gets it, can he? I can't get blood out of a turnip, can I?

MRS. BOYLE. It's nearly two months since we heard of the Will, an' the money seems as far off as ever. . . . I suppose you know we owe twenty pouns to oul' Murphy?

BOYLE. I've a faint recollection of you tellin' me that before.

MRS. BOYLE. Well, you'll go over to the shop yourself for the things in future—I'll face him no more.

BOYLE. I thought you said you were goin'?

MRS. BOYLE. I'm goin' now; come on, Mary.

BOYLE. Ey, Juno, ey!

MRS. BOYLE. Well, what d'ye want now?

BOYLE. Is there e'er a bottle o' stout left?

MRS. BOYLE. There's two o' them here still.

BOYLE. Show us in one o' them an' leave t'other there till I get up. An' throw us in the paper that's on the table, an' the bottle o' Sloan's Liniment that's in th' drawer.

MRS. BOYLE (*getting the liniment and the stout*). What paper is it you want—the *Messenger*?

BOYLE. *Messenger! The News o' the World!*

(MRS. BOYLE *brings in the things asked for and comes out again.*)

MRS. BOYLE (*at door*). Mind the candle, now, an' don't burn the house over our heads.   I left t'other bottle o' stout on the table.

> (*She puts bottle of stout on table.   She goes out with* MARY.   *A cork is heard popping inside.*)
>
> (*A pause; then outside the door is heard the voice of* JOXER *lilting softly:* "Me pipe I'll smoke, as I dhrive me moke . . . are you . . . there . . . More . . . aar . . . i . . . tee!" *A gentle knock is heard and, after a pause, the door opens, and* JOXER, *followed by* NUGENT, *enters.*)

JOXER. Be God, they must be all out; I was thinkin' there was somethin' up when he didn't answer the signal.   We seen Juno an' Mary goin', but I didn't see him, an' it's very seldom he escapes me.

NUGENT. He's not goin' to escape me—he's not goin' to be let go to the fair altogether.

JOXER. Sure, the house couldn't hould them lately; an' he goin' about like a mastherpiece of the Free State counthry; forgettin' their friends; forgettin' God—wouldn't even lift his hat passin' a chapel!   Sure they were bound to get a dhrop!   An' you really think there's no money comin' to him afther all?

NUGENT. Not as much as a red rex, man; I've been a bit anxious this long time over me money, an' I went up to the solicitor's to find out all I could—ah, man, they were goin' to throw me down the stairs. They toul' me that the oul' cock himself had the stairs worn away comin' up afther it, an' they black in the face tellin' him he'd get nothin'. Some way or another that the Will is writ he won't be entitled to get as much as a make!

JOXER. Ah, I thought there was somethin' curious about the whole thing; I've bin havin' sthrange dhreams for the last couple o' weeks. An' I notice that that Bentham fella doesn't be comin' here now—there must be somethin' on the mat there too. Anyhow, who, in the name o' God, ud leave anythin' to that oul' bummer? Sure it ud be unnatural. An' the way Juno an' him's been throwin' their weight about for the last few months! Ah, him that goes a borrowin' goes a sorrowin'!

NUGENT. Well, he's not goin' to throw his weight about in the suit I made for him much longer. I'm tellin' you seven pouns aren't to be found growin' on the bushes these days.

JOXER. An' there isn't hardly a neighbour in the whole street that hasn't lent him money

84

on the strength of what he was goin' to get,
but they're after backing the wrong horse.
Wasn't it a mercy o' God that I'd nothin' to
give him! The softy I am, you know, I'd ha'
lent him me last juice! I must have had somebody's good prayers. Ah, afther all, an honest
man's the noblest work o' God!

(BOYLE *coughs inside.*)

JOXER. Whisht, damn it, he must be inside
in bed.

NUGENT. Inside o' bed or outside of it
he's goin' to pay me for that suit, or give it
back—he'll not climb up my back as easily
as he thinks.

JOXER. Gwan in at wanst, man, an' get it
off him, an' don't be a fool.

NUGENT (*going to door left, opening it and looking in*). Ah, don't disturb yourself, Mr. Boyle;
I hope you're not sick?

BOYLE. Th' oul' legs, Mr. Nugent, the oul'
legs.

NUGENT. I just called over to see if you
could let me have anything off the suit?

BOYLE. E-e-e-eh, how much is this it is?

NUGENT. It's the same as it was at the start
—seven pouns.

BOYLE. I'm glad you kem, Mr. Nugent; I
want a good heavy top-coat—Irish frieze, if

85

you have it.   How much would a top-coat like that be, now?

NUGENT. About six pouns.

BOYLE. Six pouns—six an' seven, six an' seven is thirteen—that'll be thirteen pouns I'll owe you.

> (JOXER *slips the bottle of stout that is on the table into his pocket.* NUGENT *rushes into the room, and returns with suit on his arm; he pauses at the door.*)

NUGENT. You'll owe me no thirteen pouns. Maybe you think you're betther able to owe it than pay it!

BOYLE (*frantically*). Here, come back to hell ower that—where're you goin' with them clothes o' mine?

NUGENT. Where am I goin' with them clothes o' yours? Well, I like your damn cheek!

BOYLE. Here, what am I goin' to dhress meself in when I'm goin' out?

NUGENT. What do I care what you dhress yourself in!   You can put yourself in a bolsther cover, if you like.

> (*He goes towards the other door, followed by* JOXER.)

JOXER. What'll he dhress himself in! Gentleman Jack an' his frieze coat!

> (*They go out.*)

BOYLE (*inside*). Ey, Nugent; ey, Mr. Nugent, Mr. Nugent!

> (*After a pause* BOYLE *enters hastily, buttoning the braces of his moleskin trousers; his coat and vest are on his arm; he throws these on a chair and hurries to the door on right.*)

BOYLE. Ey, Mr. Nugent, Mr. Nugent!

JOXER (*meeting him at the door*). What's up, what's wrong, Captain?

BOYLE. Nugent's been here an' took away me suit—the only things I had to go out in!

JOXER. Tuk your suit—for God's sake! An' what were you doin' while he was takin' them?

BOYLE. I was in bed when he stole in like a thief in the night, an' before I knew even what he was thinkin' of, he whipped them from the chair, an' was off like a redshank!

JOXER. An' what, in the name o' God, did he do that for?

BOYLE. What did he do it for? How the hell do I know what he done it for?—jealousy an' spite, I suppose.

JOXER. Did he not say what he done it for?

BOYLE. Amn't I afther tellin' you that he had them whipped up an' was gone before I could open me mouth?

JOXER. That was a very sudden thing to do; there mus' be somethin' behin' it. Did he hear anythin', I wondher?

BOYLE. Did he hear anythin'?—you talk very queer, Joxer—what could he hear?

JOXER. About you not gettin' the money, in some way or t'other?

BOYLE. An' what ud prevent me from gettin' th' money?

JOXER. That's jus' what I was thinkin'—what ud prevent you from gettin' the money—nothin', as far as I can see.

BOYLE (*looking round for bottle of stout, with an exclamation*). Aw, holy God!

JOXER. What's up, Jack?

BOYLE. He must have afther lifted the bottle o' stout that Juno left on the table!

JOXER (*horrified*). Ah no, ah no; he wouldn't be afther doin' that now.

BOYLE. An' who done it then? Juno left a bottle o' stout here, an' it's gone—it didn't walk, did it?

JOXER. Oh, that's shockin'; ah, man's inhumanity to man makes countless thousands mourn!

MRS. MADIGAN (*appearing at the door*). I hope I'm not disturbin' you in any discussion on your forthcomin' legacy—if I may use the word—an' that you'll let me have a barny for a minute or two with you, Mr. Boyle.

BOYLE (*uneasily*). To be sure, Mrs. Madigan —an oul' friend's always welcome.

JOXER. Come in the evenin', come in th' mornin'; come when you're assed, or come without warnin', Mrs. Madigan.

BOYLE. Sit down, Mrs. Madigan.

MRS. MADIGAN (*ominously*). Th' few words I have to say can be said standin'. Puttin' aside all formularies, I suppose you remember me lendin' you some time ago three pouns that I raised on blankets an' furniture in me uncle's?

BOYLE. I remember it well. I have it recorded in me book—three pouns five shillins from Maisie Madigan, raised on articles pawned; an', item: fourpence, given to make up the price of a pint, on th' principle that no bird ever flew on wan wing; all to be repaid at par, when the ship comes home.

MRS. MADIGAN. Well, ever since I shoved in the blankets I've been perishing with th' cowld, an' I've decided, if I'll be too hot in th' nex' world aself, I'm not goin' to be too cowld in this wan; an' consequently, I want me three pouns, if you please.

BOYLE. This is a very sudden demand, Mrs.

Madigan, an' can't be met; but I'm willin' to
give you a receipt in full, in full.

MRS. MADIGAN. Come on, out with th'
money, an' don't be jack-actin'.

BOYLE. You can't get blood out of a turnip,
can you?

MRS. MADIGAN (*rushing over and shaking him*).
Gimme me money, y'oul' reprobate, or I'll
shake the worth of it out of you!

BOYLE. Ey, houl' on, there; houl' on, there!
You'll wait for your money now, me lassie!

MRS. MADIGAN (*looking around the room and
seeing the gramophone*). I'll wait for it, will I?
Well, I'll not wait long; if I can't get th' cash,
I'll get th' worth of it.

(*She catches up the gramophone.*)

BOYLE. Ey, ey, there, wher'r you goin' with
that?

MRS. MADIGAN. I'm goin' to th' pawn to
get me three quid five shillins; I'll brin' you
th' ticket, an' then you can do what you like,
me bucko.

BOYLE. You can't touch that, you can't
touch that! It's not my property, an' it's not
ped for yet!

MRS. MADIGAN. So much th' bether. It'll
be an ayse to me conscience, for I'm takin'
what doesn't belong to you. You're not goin'

to be swankin' it like a paycock with Maisie Madigan's money—I'll pull some o' th' gorgeous feathers out o' your tail!

(*She goes off with the gramophone.*)

BOYLE. What's th' world comin' to at all? I ass you, Joxer Daly, is there any morality left anywhere?

JOXER. I wouldn't ha' believed it, only I seen it with me own two eyes.   I didn't think Maisie Madigan was that sort of a woman; she has either a sup taken, or she's heard somethin'.

BOYLE. Heard somethin'—about what, if it's not any harm to ass you?

JOXER. She must ha' heard some rumour or other that you weren't goin' to get th' money.

BOYLE. Who says I'm not goin' to get th' money?

JOXER. Sure, I know—I was only sayin'.

BOYLE. Only sayin' what?

JOXER. Nothin'.

BOYLE. You were goin' to say somethin', don't be a twisther.

JOXER (*angrily*). Who's a twisther?

BOYLE. Why don't you speak your mind, then?

JOXER. You never twisted yourself—no, you wouldn't know how!

BOYLE. Did you ever know me to twist; did you ever know me to twist?

JOXER (*fiercely*). Did you ever do anythin' else! Sure, you can't believe a word that comes out o' your mouth.

BOYLE. Here, get out, ower o' this; I always knew you were a prognosticator an' a procrastinator!

JOXER (*going out as* JOHNNY *comes in*). The anchor's weighed, farewell, ree . . . mem . . . ber . . . me. Jacky Boyle, Esquire, infernal rogue an' damned liar!

JOHNNY. Joxer an' you at it agen?—when are you goin' to have a little respect for yourself, an' not be always makin' a show of us all?

BOYLE. Are you goin' to lecture me now?

JOHNNY. Is mother back from the doctor yet, with Mary?

(MRS. BOYLE *enters; it is apparent from the serious look on her face that something has happened. She takes off her hat and coat without a word and puts them by. She then sits down near the fire, and there is a few moments' pause.*)

BOYLE. Well, what did the doctor say about Mary?

MRS. BOYLE (*in an earnest manner and*

with suppressed agitation). Sit down here, Jack; I've something to say to you . . . about Mary.

BOYLE (*awed by her manner*). About . . . Mary?

MRS. BOYLE. Close that door there and sit down here.

BOYLE (*closing the door*). More throuble in our native land, is it? (*He sits down*) Well, what is it?

MRS. BOYLE. It's about Mary.

BOYLE. Well, what about Mary—there's nothin' wrong with her, is there?

MRS. BOYLE. I'm sorry to say there's a gradle wrong with her.

BOYLE. A gradle wrong with her! (*Peevishly*) First Johnny an' now Mary; is the whole house goin' to become an hospital! It's not consumption, is it?

MRS. BOYLE. No . . . it's not consumption . . . it's worse.

JOHNNY. Worse! Well, we'll have to get her into some place ower this, there's no one here to mind her.

MRS. BOYLE. We'll all have to mind her now. You might as well know now, Johnny, as another time. (*To* BOYLE) D'ye know what the doctor said to me about her, Jack?

93

BOYLE. How ud I know—I wasn't there, was I?

MRS. BOYLE. He told me to get her married at wanst.

BOYLE. Married at wanst! An' why did he say the like o' that?

MRS. BOYLE. Because Mary's goin' to have a baby in a short time.

BOYLE. Goin' to have a baby!—my God, what'll Bentham say when he hears that?

MRS. BOYLE. Are you blind, man, that you can't see that it was Bentham that has done this wrong to her?

BOYLE (*passionately*). Then he'll marry her, he'll have to marry her!

MRS. BOYLE. You know he's gone to England, an' God knows where he is now.

BOYLE. I'll folly him, I'll folly him, an' bring him back, an' make him do her justice. The scoundrel, I might ha' known what he was, with his yogees an' his prawna!

MRS. BOYLE. We'll have to keep it quiet till we see what we can do.

BOYLE. Oh, isn't this a nice thing to come on top o' me, an' the state I'm in! A pretty show I'll be to Joxer an' to that oul' wan, Madigan! Amn't I afther goin' through enough without havin' to go throvgh this!

MRS. BOYLE. What you an' I'll have to go through'll be nothin' to what poor Mary'll have to go through; for you an' me is middlin' old, an' most of our years is spent; but Mary'll have maybe forty years to face an' handle, an' every wan of them'll be tainted with a bitther memory.

BOYLE. Where is she? Where is she till I tell her off? I'm tellin' you when I'm done with her she'll be a sorry girl!

MRS. BOYLE. I left her in me sisther's till I came to speak to you. You'll say nothin' to her, Jack; ever since she left school she's earned her livin', an' your fatherly care never throubled the poor girl.

BOYLE. Gwan, take her part agen her father! But I'll let you see whether I'll say nothin' to her or no! Her an' her readin'! That's more o' th' blasted nonsense that has the house fallin' down on top of us! What did th' likes of her, born in a tenement house, want with readin'? Her readin's afther bringin' her to a nice pass—oh, it's madnin', madnin', madnin'!

MRS. BOYLE. When she comes back say nothin' to her, Jack, or she'll leave this place.

BOYLE. Leave this place! Ay, she'll leave this place, an' quick too!

MRS. BOYLE. If Mary goes, I'll go with her.

BOYLE. Well, go with her! Well, go, th' pair o' yous! I lived before I seen yous, an' I can live when yous are gone. Isn't this a nice thing to come rollin' in on top o' me afther all your prayin' to St. Anthony an' The Little Flower. An' she's a child o' Mary, too—I wonder what'll the nuns think of her now? An' it'll be bellows'd all over th' disthrict before you could say Jack Robinson; an' whenever I'm seen they'll whisper, " That's th' father of Mary Boyle that had th' kid be th' swank she used to go with; d'ye know, d'ye know?" To be sure they'll know—more about it than I will meself!

JOHNNY. She should be dhriven out o' th' house she's brought disgrace on!

MRS. BOYLE. Hush, you, Johnny. We needn't let it be bellows'd all over the place; all we've got to do is to leave this place quietly an' go somewhere where we're not known, an' nobody'll be th' wiser.

BOYLE. You're talkin' like a two-year-oul', woman. Where'll we get a place ou' o' this?— places aren't that easily got.

MRS. BOYLE. But, Jack, when we get the money . . .

BOYLE. Money—what money?

MRS. BOYLE. Why, oul' Ellison's money, of course.

BOYLE. There's no money comin' from oul' Ellison, or any one else.   Since you've heard of wan throuble, you might as well hear of another.   There's no money comin' to us at all—the Will's a wash out!

MRS. BOYLE. What are you sayin', man—no money?

JOHNNY. How could it be a wash out?

BOYLE. The boyo that's afther doin' it to Mary done it to me as well.   The thick made out the Will wrong; he said in th' Will, only first cousin an' second cousin, instead of mentionin' our names, an' now any one that thinks he's a first cousin or second cousin t'oul' Ellison can claim the money as well as me, an' they're springin' up in hundreds, an' comin' from America an' Australia, thinkin' to get their whack out of it, while all the time the lawyers is gobblin' it up, till there's not as much as ud buy a stockin' for your lovely daughter's baby!

MRS. BOYLE. I don't believe it, I don't believe it, I don't believe it!

JOHNNY. Why did you say nothin' about this before?

MRS. BOYLE. You're not serious, Jack; you're not serious!

BOYLE. I'm tellin' you the scholar, Bentham, made a banjax o' th' Will; instead o' sayin', "th' rest o' me property to be divided between me first cousin, Jack Boyle, an' me second cousin, Mick Finnegan, o' Santhry", he writ down only, "me first an' second cousins", an' the world an' his wife are afther th' property now.

MRS. BOYLE. Now, I know why Bentham left poor Mary in th' lurch; I can see it all now—oh, is there not even a middlin' honest man left in th' world?

JOHNNY (*to* BOYLE). An' you let us run into debt, an' you borreyed money from everybody to fill yourself with beer! An' now, you tell us the whole thing's a wash out! Oh, if it's thrue, I'm done with you, for you're worse than me sisther Mary!

BOYLE. You hole your tongue, d'ye hear? I'll not take any lip from you. Go an' get Bentham if you want satisfaction for all that's afther happenin' us.

JOHNNY. I won't hole me tongue, I won't hole me tongue! I'll tell you what I think of you, father an' all as you are . . . you . . .

MRS. BOYLE. Johnny, Johnny, Johnny, for God's sake, be quiet!

98

JOHNNY. I'll not be quiet, I'll not be quiet; he's a nice father, isn't he?   Is it any wondher Mary went asthray, when . . .

MRS. BOYLE. Johnny, Johnny, for my sake be quiet—for your mother's sake!

BOYLE. I'm goin' out now to have a few dhrinks with th' last few makes I have, an' tell that lassie o' yours not to be here when I come back; for if I lay me eyes on her, I'll lay me hans on her, an' if I lay me hans on her, I won't be accountable for me actions!

JOHNNY. Take care somebody doesn't lay his hans on you—y'oul' . . .

MRS. BOYLE. Johnny, Johnny!

BOYLE (*at door, about to go out*). Oh, a nice son, an' a nicer daughter, I have. (*Calling loudly upstairs*) Joxer, Joxer, are you there?

JOXER (*from a distance*). I'm here, More . . . ee . . . aar . . . i . . . tee!

BOYLE. I'm goin' down to Foley's—are you comin'?

JOXER. Come with you?   With that sweet call me heart is stirred; I'm only waiting for the word, an' I'll be with you, like a bird!

(BOYLE *and* JOXER *pass the door going out.*)

JOHNNY (*throwing himself on the bed*). I've a nice sisther, an' a nice father, there's no bettin' on it.   I wish to God a bullet or a bomb

99

had whipped me ou' o' this long ago! Not one o' yous, not one o' yous, have any thought for me!

MRS. BOYLE (*with passionate remonstrance*). If you don't whisht, Johnny, you'll drive me mad. Who has kep' th' home together for the past few years—only me. An' who'll have to bear th' biggest part o' this throuble but me— but whinin' an' whingin' isn't goin' to do any good.

JOHNNY. You're to blame yourself for a gradle of it—givin' him his own way in everything, an' never assin' to check him, no matther what he done. Why didn't you look afther th' money? why . . .

(*There is a knock at the door*; MRS. BOYLE *opens it*; JOHNNY *rises on his elbow to look and listen; two men enter.*)

FIRST MAN. We've been sent up be th' Manager of the Hibernian Furnishing Co., Mrs. Boyle, to take back the furniture that was got a while ago.

MRS. BOYLE. Yous'll touch nothin' here— how do I know who yous are?

FIRST MAN (*showing a paper*). There's the ordher, ma'am. (*Reading*) A chest o' drawers, a table, wan easy an' two ordinary chairs; wan mirror; wan chestherfield divan, an' a wardrobe an' two vases. (*To his comrade*) Come on, Bill, it's afther knockin' off time already.

JOHNNY. For God's sake, mother, run down to Foley's an' bring father back, or we'll be left without a stick.

(*The men carry out the table.*)

MRS. BOYLE. What good would it be—you heard what he said before he went out.

JOHNNY. Can't you thry; he ought to be here, an' the like of this goin' on.

(MRS. BOYLE *puts a shawl around her, as* MARY *enters.*)

MARY. What's up, mother? I met men carryin' away the table, an' everybody's talking about us not gettin' the money after all.

MRS. BOYLE. Everythin's gone wrong, Mary, everythin'. We're not gettin' a penny out o' the Will, not a penny—I'll tell you all when I come back; I'm goin' for your father. (*She runs out.*)

JOHNNY (*to* MARY, *who has sat down by the fire*). It's a wondher you're not ashamed to show your face here, afther what has happened.

(JERRY *enters slowly; there is a look of earnest hope on his face. He looks at* MARY *for a few moments.*)

JERRY (*softly*). Mary!

(MARY *does not answer.*)

JERRY. Mary, I want to speak to you for a few moments, may I?

(MARY *remains silent;* JOHNNY *goes slowly into room on left.*)

JERRY. Your mother has told me everything, Mary, and I have come to you. . . . I have come to tell you, Mary, that my love for you is greater and deeper than ever. . . .

MARY (*with a sob*). Oh, Jerry, Jerry, say no more; all that is over now; anything like that is impossible now!

JERRY. Impossible? Why do you talk like that, Mary?

MARY. After all that has happened.

JERRY. What does it matter what has happened? We are young enough to be able to forget all those things. (*He catches her hand*) Mary, Mary, I am pleading for your love. With Labour, Mary, humanity is above everything; we are the Leaders in the fight for a new life. I want to forget Bentham, I want to forget that you left me—even for a while.

MARY. Oh, Jerry, Jerry, you haven't the bitter word of scorn for me after all.

JERRY (*passionately*). Scorn! I love you, love you, Mary!

MARY (*rising, and looking him in the eyes*). Even though . . .

JERRY. Even though you threw me over for another man; even though you gave me many a bitter word!

MARY. Yes, yes, I know; but you love me, even though . . . even though . . . I'm . . . goin' . . . goin' . . . (*He looks at her questioningly, and fear gathers in his eyes.*) Ah, I was thinkin' so. . . . You don't know everything!

JERRY (*poignantly*). Surely to God, Mary, you don't mean that . . . that . . . that . . .

MARY. Now you know all, Jerry; now you know all!

JERRY. My God, Mary, have you fallen as low as that?

MARY. Yes, Jerry, as you say, I have fallen as low as that.

JERRY. I didn't mean it that way, Mary . . . it came on me so sudden, that I didn't mind what I was sayin'. . . . I never expected this —you're mother never told me. . . . I'm sorry . . . God knows, I'm sorry for you, Mary.

MARY. Let us say no more, Jerry; I don't blame you for thinkin' it's terrible. . . . I suppose it is. . . . Everybody'll think the same . . . it's only as I expected — your humanity is just as narrow as the humanity of the others.

JERRY. I'm sorry, all the same. . . . I shouldn't have troubled you. . . . I wouldn't if I'd known. . . . If I can do anything for you . . . Mary . . . I will. (*He turns to go, and halts at the door.*)

MARY. Do you remember, Jerry, the verses you read when you gave the lecture in the Socialist Rooms some time ago, on Humanity's Strife with Nature?

JERRY. The verses—no; I don't remember them.

MARY. I do. They're runnin' in me head now—

> An' we felt the power that fashion'd
> All the lovely things we saw,
> That created all the murmur
> Of an everlasting law,
> Was a hand of force an' beauty,
> With an eagle's tearin' claw.
>
> Then we saw our globe of beauty
> Was an ugly thing as well,
> A hymn divine whose chorus
> Was an agonizin' yell;
> Like the story of a demon,
> That an angel had to tell;
>
> Like a glowin' picture by a
> Hand unsteady, brought to ruin;

Like her craters, if their deadness
Could give life unto the moon;
Like the agonizing horror
Of a violin out of tune.

(*There is a pause, and* DEVINE *goes slowly
out.*)

JOHNNY (*returning*). Is he gone?

MARY. Yes.

(*The two men re-enter.*)

FIRST MAN. We can't wait any longer for
t'oul' fella—sorry, Miss, but we have to live
as well as th' nex' man.

(*They carry out some things.*)

JOHNNY. Oh, isn't this terrible! . . . I
suppose you told him everything . . . couldn't
you have waited for a few days . . . he'd have
stopped th' takin' of the things, if you'd kep
your mouth shut. Are you burnin' to tell
every one of the shame you've brought on us?

MARY (*snatching up her hat and coat*). Oh,
this is unbearable!   (*She rushes out.*)

FIRST MAN (*re-entering*). We'll take the chest
o' drawers next—it's the heaviest.

(*The votive light flickers for a moment,
and goes out.*)

JOHNNY (*in a cry of fear*). Mother o' God,
the light's afther goin' out!

FIRST MAN. You put the win' up me the

way you bawled that time.   The oil's all gone, that's all.

JOHNNY (*with an agonizing cry*). Mother o' God, there's a shot I'm after gettin'!

FIRST MAN. What's wrong with you, man? Is it a fit you're takin'?

JOHNNY. I'm after feelin' a pain in me breast, like the tearin' by of a bullet!

FIRST MAN. He's goin' mad—it's a wondher they'd leave a chap like that here be himself.

(*Two* IRREGULARS *enter swiftly; they carry revolvers; one goes over to* JOHNNY; *the other covers the two furniture men.*)

FIRST IRREGULAR (*to the men, quietly and incisively*). Who are you—what are yous doin' here—quick!

FIRST MAN. Removin' furniture that's not paid for.

IRREGULAR. Get over to the other end of the room an' turn your faces to the wall—quick.

(*The two men turn their faces to the wall, with their hands up.*)

SECOND IRREGULAR (*to* JOHNNY). Come on, Sean Boyle, you're wanted; some of us have a word to say to you.

JOHNNY. I'm sick, I can't—what do you want with me?

SECOND IRREGULAR. Come on, come on;

we've a distance to go, an' haven't much time
—come on.

JOHNNY. I'm an oul' comrade — yous
wouldn't shoot an oul' comrade.

SECOND IRREGULAR. Poor Tancred was an
oul' comrade o' yours, but you didn't think o'
that when you gave him away to the gang that
sent him to his grave. But we've no time to
waste; come on—here, Dermot, ketch his
arm. (*To* JOHNNY) Have you your beads?

JOHNNY. Me beads! Why do you ass me
that, why do you ass me that?

SECOND IRREGULAR. Go on, go on, march!

JOHNNY. Are yous goin' to do in a comrade
—look at me arm, I lost it for Ireland.

SECOND IRREGULAR. Commandant Tancred
lost his life for Ireland.

JOHNNY. Sacred Heart of Jesus, have mercy
on me! Mother o' God pray for me—be with
me now in the agonies o' death! . . . Hail, Mary,
full o' grace . . . the Lord is . . . with Thee.

> (*They drag out* JOHNNY BOYLE, *and the
> curtain falls. When it rises again the
> most of the furniture is gone.* MARY
> *and* MRS. BOYLE, *one on each side, are
> sitting in a darkened room, by the fire;
> it is an hour later.*)

MRS. BOYLE. I'll not wait much longer . . .

what did they bring him away in the mothor
for?   Nugent says he thinks they had guns
. . . is me throubles never goin' to be over?
. . . If anything ud happen to poor Johnny,
I think I'd lose me mind. . . . I'll go to the
Police Station, surely they ought to be able to
do somethin'.

(*Below is heard the sound of voices.*)

MRS. BOYLE. Whisht, is that something?
Maybe, it's your father, though when I left
him in Foley's he was hardly able to lift his
head.   Whisht!

(*A knock at the door, and the voice of*
MRS. MADIGAN, *speaking very softly*):
Mrs. Boyle, Mrs. Boyle.

(MRS. BOYLE *opens the door*.)

MRS. MADIGAN. Oh, Mrs. Boyle, God an'
His Blessed Mother be with you this night!

MRS. BOYLE (*calmly*). What is it, Mrs.
Madigan?   It's Johnny—something about
Johnny.

MRS. MADIGAN. God send it's not, God send
it's not Johnny!

MRS. BOYLE. Don't keep me waitin', Mrs.
Madigan; I've gone through so much lately
that I feel able for anything.

MRS. MADIGAN. Two polismen below wantin'
you.

MRS. BOYLE. Wantin' me; an' why do they want me?

MRS. MADIGAN. Some poor fella's been found, an' they think it's, it's . . .

MRS. BOYLE. Johnny, Johnny!

MARY (*with her arms round her mother*). Oh, mother, mother, me poor, darlin' mother.

MRS. BOYLE. Hush, hush, darlin'; you'll shortly have your own throuble to bear. (*To* MRS. MADIGAN) An' why do the polis think it's Johnny, Mrs. Madigan?

MRS. MADIGAN. Because one o' the doctors knew him when he was attendin' with his poor arm.

MRS. BOYLE. Oh, it's thrue, then; it's Johnny, it's me son, me own son!

MARY. Oh, it's thrue, it's thrue what Jerry Devine says—there isn't a God, there isn't a God; if there was He wouldn't let these things happen!

MRS. BOYLE. Mary, Mary, you musn't say them things. We'll want all the help we can get from God an' His Blessed Mother now! These things have nothin' to do with the Will o' God. Ah, what can God do agen the stupidity o' men!

MRS. MADIGAN. The polis want you to go with them to the hospital to see the poor body —they're waitin' below.

MRS. BOYLE. We'll go. Come, Mary, an' we'll never come back here agen. Let your father furrage for himself now; I've done all I could an' it was all no use—he'll be hopeless till the end of his days. I've got a little room in me sisther's where we'll stop till your throuble is over, an' then we'll work together for the sake of the baby.

MARY. My poor little child that'll have no father!

MRS. BOYLE. It'll have what's far betther— it'll have two mothers.

(*A rough voice shouting from below*): Are yous goin' to keep us waitin' for yous all night?

MRS. MADIGAN (*going to the door, and shouting down*). Take your hour, there, take your hour! If yous are in such a hurry, skip off, then, for nobody wants you here—if they did yous wouldn't be found. For you're the same as yous were undher the British Government— never where yous are wanted! As far as I can see, the Polis as Polis, in this city, is Null an' Void!

MRS. BOYLE. We'll go, Mary, we'll go; you to see your poor dead brother, an' me to see me poor dead son!

MARY. I dhread it, mother, I dhread it!

MRS. BOYLE. I forgot, Mary, I forgot; your poor oul' selfish mother was only thinkin' of herself. No, no, you musn't come—it wouldn't be good for you. You go on to me sisther's an' I'll face th' ordeal meself. Maybe I didn't feel sorry enough for Mrs. Tancred when her poor son was found as Johnny's been found now—because he was a Die-hard! Ah, why didn't I remember that then he wasn't a Die-hard or a Stater, but only a poor dead son! It's well I remember all that she said—an' it's my turn to say it now: What was the pain I suffered, Johnny, bringin' you into the world to carry you to your cradle to the pains I'll suffer carryin' you out o' the world to bring you to your grave! Mother o' God, Mother o' God, have pity on us all! Blessed Virgin, where were you when me darlin' son was riddled with bullets, when me darlin' son was riddled with bullets? Sacred Heart o' Jesus, take away our hearts o' stone, and give us hearts o' flesh! Take away this murdherin' hate, an' give us Thine own eternal love!

(*They all go slowly out.*)

(*There is a pause; then a sound of shuffling steps on the stairs outside. The door opens and* BOYLE *and* JOXER, *both of them very drunk, enter.*)

III

BOYLE. I'm able to go no farther. . . . Two polis, ey . . . what were they doin' here, I wondher? . . . Up to no good, anyhow . . . an' Juno an' that lovely daughter o' mine with them. (*Taking a sixpence from his pocket and looking at it*) Wan single, solitary tanner left out of all I borreyed. . . . (*He lets it fall.*) The last o' the Mohicans. . . . The blinds is down, Joxer, the blinds is down!

JOXER (*walking unsteadily across the room, and anchoring at the bed*). Put all . . . your throubles . . . in your oul' kit bag . . . an' smile . . . smile . . . smile!

BOYLE. The counthry'll have to steady itself . . . it's goin' . . . to hell. . . . Where'r all . . . the chairs . . . gone to . . . steady itself, Joxer. . . . Chairs'll . . . have to . . . steady themselves. . . . No matther . . . what any one may . . . say. . . . Irelan' sober . . . is Irelan' . . . free.

JOXER (*stretching himself on the bed*). Chains . . . an' . . . slaveree . . . that's a darlin' motto . . . a daaarlin' . . . motto!

BOYLE. If th' worst comes . . . to th' worse . . . I can join a . . . flyin' . . . column. . . . I done . . . me bit . . . in Easther Week . . . had no business . . . to . . . be . . . there . . . but Captain Boyle's Captain Boyle!

JOXER. Breathes there a man with soul . . . so . . . de . . . ad . . . this . . . me . . . o . . . wn, me nat . . . ive l . . . an'!

BOYLE (*subsiding into a sitting posture on the floor*). Commandant Kelly died . . . in them . . . arms . . . Joxer. . . . Tell me Volunteer Butties . . . says he . . . that . . . I died for . . . Irelan'!

JOXER. D'jever rade Willie . . . Reilly . . . an' his . . . own . . . Colleen . . . Bawn? It's a darlin' story, a daarlin' story!

BOYLE. I'm telling you . . . Joxer . . . th' whole worl's . . . in a terr . . . ible state o' . . . chassis!

CURTAIN

The Shadow of a Gunman was first produced in the Abbey Theatre, Dublin, on April the 12th, 1923, with the following cast:

DONAL DAVOREN	.	.	.	. Arthur Shields
SEUMAS SHIELDS .	.	.	.	. F. J. McCormick
TOMMY OWENS .	.	.	.	. Michael J. Dolan
ADOLPHUS GRIGSON	.	.	.	. P. J. Carolan
MRS. GRIGSON .	.	.	.	. May Craig
MINNIE POWELL	.	.	.	. Gertrude Murphy
MR. MULLIGAN .	.	.	.	Eric Gorman
MR. MAGUIRE .	.	.	.	. G. V. Lavelle
MRS. HENDERSON	.	.	.	. Christine Hayden
MR. GALLOGHER	.	.	.	. Gabriel J. Fallon
AN AUXILIARY .	.	.	.	. Tony Quinn

THE
SHADOW OF A GUNMAN
A Tragedy in Two Acts

THE CHARACTERS IN THE PLAY

Donal Davoren
Seumas Shields, *a pedlar*
Tommy Owens
Adolphus Grigson
Mrs. Grigson
Minnie Powell
} *Residents in the Tenement.*

Mr. Mulligan, *the landlord.*
Mr. Maguire, *soldier of the I.R.A.*
Mrs. Henderson
Mr. Gallogher
} *Residents of an adjoining Tenement.*
An Auxiliary.

SCENE

A room in a tenement in Hilljoy Square, Dublin.

Some hours elapse between the two acts. The period of the Play is May 1920.

ACT I

Scene: *A Return Room in a tenement house in Hilljoy Square. At the back two large windows looking out into the yard; they occupy practically the whole of the back wall space. Between the windows is a cupboard, on the top of which is a pile of books. The doors are open, and on these are hanging a number of collars and ties. Running parallel with the windows is a stretcher bed; another runs at right angles along the wall at right. At the head of this bed is a door leading to the rest of the house. The wall on the left runs diagonally, so that the fireplace—which is in the centre—is plainly visible. On the mantelshelf to the right is a statue of the Virgin, to the left a statue of the Sacred Heart, and in the centre a crucifix. Around the fireplace are a few common cooking utensils. In the centre of the room is a table, on which are a typewriter, a candle and*

117

candlestick, a bunch of wild flowers in a vase, writing materials and a number of books. There are two chairs, one near the fireplace and one at the table. The aspect of the place is one of absolute untidiness, engendered on the one hand by the congenital slovenliness of SEUMAS SHIELDS, *and on the other by the temperament of* DONAL DAVOREN, *making it appear impossible to effect an improvement in such a place.*

DAVOREN *is sitting at the table typing. He is about thirty. There is in his face an expression that seems to indicate an eternal war between weakness and strength; there is in the lines of the brow and chin an indication of a desire for activity, while in his eyes there is visible an unquenchable tendency towards rest. His struggle through life has been a hard one, and his efforts have been handicapped by an inherited and self-developed devotion to " the might of design, the mystery of colour and the belief in the redemption of all things by beauty everlasting ". His life would drive him mad were it not for the fact that he never knew any other. He bears upon his body the marks of the struggle for existence and the efforts towards self-expression.*

118

SEUMAS SHIELDS, *who is in the bed next the wall to the right, is a heavily built man of thirty-five; he is dark-haired and sallow-complexioned. In him is frequently manifested the superstition, the fear and the malignity of primitive man.*

DAVOREN (*lilting an air as he composes*):

Or when sweet Summer's ardent arms outspread
Entwined with flowers,
Enfold us, like two lovers newly wed,
Thro' ravish'd hours—
Then sorrow, woe and pain lose all their powers,
For each is dead, and life is only ours.

(*A woman's figure appears at the window and taps loudly on one of the panes; at the same moment there is loud knocking at the door.*)

VOICE OF WOMAN AT WINDOW. Are you awake, Mr. Shields — Mr. Shields, are you awake? Are you goin' to get up to-day at all, at all?

VOICE AT THE DOOR. Mr. Shields, is there any use of callin' you at all? This is a nice nine o'clock: do you know what time it is, Mr. Shields?

SEUMAS (*loudly*). Yus!

VOICE AT THE DOOR. Why don't you get up, then, an' not have the house turned into a bedlam tryin' to waken you?

SEUMAS (*shouting*). Alright, alright, alright! The way these oul' ones bawl at a body! Upon my soul! I'm beginnin' to believe that the Irish People are still in the stone age. If they could they'd throw a bomb at you.

DAVOREN. A land mine exploding under the bed is the only thing that would lift you out of it.

SEUMAS (*stretching himself*). Oh-h-h. I was fast in the arms of Morpheus—he was one of the infernal deities, son of Somnos, wasn't he?

DAVOREN. I think so.

SEUMAS. The poppy was his emblem, wasn't it?

DAVOREN. Ah, I don't know.

SEUMAS. It's a bit cold this morning, I think, isn't it?

DAVOREN. It's quite plain I'm not going to get much quietness in this house.

SEUMAS (*after a pause*). I wonder what time is it?

DAVOREN. The Angelus went some time ago.

SEUMAS (*sitting up in bed suddenly*). The Angelus! It couldn't be that late, could it? I asked them to call me at nine so that I could get Mass before I went on my rounds. Why didn't you give us a rap?

DAVOREN. Give you a rap! Why, man, they've been thundering at the door and hammering at the window for the past two hours, till the house shook to its very foundations, but you took less notice of the infernal din than I would take of the strumming of a grasshopper.

SEUMAS. There's no fear of you thinking of any one else when you're at your poetry. The land of Saints and Scholars 'ill shortly be a land of bloody poets. (*Anxiously*) I suppose Maguire has come and gone?

DAVOREN. Maguire? No, he hasn't been here—why, did you expect him?

SEUMAS (*in a burst of indignation*). He said he'd be here at nine. " Before the last chime has struck," says he, " I'll be coming in on the door," and it must be—what time is it now?

DAVOREN. Oh, it must be half-past twelve.

SEUMAS. Did anybody ever see the like of the Irish People? Is there any use of tryin' to do anything in this country? Have everything packed and ready, have everything packed and ready, have . . .

DAVOREN. And have you everything packed and ready?

SEUMAS. What's the use of having anything packed and ready when he didn't come? (*He rises and dresses himself*.) No wonder this unfortunate country is as it is, for you can't depend upon the word of a single individual in it.   I suppose he was too damn lazy to get up; he wanted the streets to be well aired first.—Oh, Kathleen Ni Houlihan, your way's a thorny way.

DAVOREN.   Ah me! alas, pain, pain ever, for ever!

SEUMAS. That's from Shelley's *Prometheus Unbound*.   I could never agree with Shelley, not that there's anything to be said against him as a poet—as a poet—but . . .

DAVOREN. He flung a few stones through stained-glass windows.

SEUMAS. He wasn't the first nor he won't be the last to do that, but the stained-glass windows—more than ever of them—are here still, and Shelley is doing a jazz dance down below. (*He gives a snarling laugh of pleasure*.)

DAVOREN (*shocked*). And you actually rejoice and are exceedingly glad that, as you believe, Shelley, the sensitive, high-minded, noble-hearted Shelley, is suffering the tortures of the damned.

SEUMAS. I rejoice in the vindication of the Church and Truth.

DAVOREN. Bah.   You know as little about truth as anybody else, and you care as little about the Church as the least of those that profess her faith; your religion is simply the state of being afraid that God will torture your soul in the next world as you are afraid the Black and Tans will torture your body in this.

SEUMAS. Go on, me boy; I'll have a right laugh at you when both of us are dead.

DAVOREN. You're welcome to laugh as much as you like at me when both of us are dead.

SEUMAS (*as he is about to put on his collar and tie*). I don't think I need to wash meself this morning; do I look all right?

DAVOREN. Oh, you're all right; it's too late now to start washing yourself.   Didn't you wash yourself yesterday morning?

SEUMAS. I gave meself a great rub yesterday. (*He proceeds to pack various articles into an attaché case—spoons, forks, laces, thread, etc.*)   I think I'll bring out a few of the braces too; damn it, they're well worth sixpence each; there's great stuff in them—did you see them?

DAVOREN. Yes, you showed them to me before.

SEUMAS. They're great value; I only hope I'll be able to get enough o' them.   I'm wearing a pair of them meself—they'd do

123

Cuchullian, they're so strong. (*Counting the spoons*) There's a dozen in each of these parcels —three, six, nine—damn it, there's only eleven in this one. I better try another. Three, six, nine—my God, there's only eleven in this one too, and one of them bent! Now I suppose I'll have to go through the whole bloody lot of them, for I'd never be easy in me mind thinkin' there'd be more than a dozen in some o' them. And still we're looking for freedom —ye gods, it's a glorious country! (*He lets one fall, which he stoops to pick up.*) Oh, my God, there's the braces after breakin'.

DAVOREN. That doesn't look as if they were strong enough for Cuchullian.

SEUMAS. I put a heavy strain on them too sudden. There's that fellow Maguire never turned up, either; he's almost too lazy to wash himself. (*As he is struggling with the braces the door is hastily shoved in and* MAGUIRE *rushes in with a handbag.*) This is a nice nine o'clock. What's the use of you coming at this hour o' the day? Do you think we're going to work be moonlight? If you weren't goin' to come at nine couldn't you say you weren't. . . .

MAGUIRE. Keep your hair on; I just blew in to tell you that I couldn't go to-day at all. I have to go to Knocksedan.

124

SEUMAS. Knocksedan! An' what, in the name o' God, is bringin' you to Knocksedan?

MAGUIRE. Business, business. I'm going out to catch butterflies.

SEUMAS. If you want to make a cod of anybody, make a cod of somebody else, an' don't be tryin' to make a cod o' me. Here I've had everything packed an' ready for hours; you were to be here at nine, an' you wait till just one o'clock to come rushin' in like a mad bull to say you've got to go to Knocksedan! Can't you leave Knocksedan till to-morrow?

MAGUIRE. Can't be did, can't be did, Seumas; if I waited till to-morrow all the butterflies might be dead. I'll leave this bag here till this evening. (*He puts the bag in a corner of the room.*) Good-by . . . ee.

(*He is gone before* SEUMAS *is aware of it.*)

SEUMAS (*with a gesture of despair*). Oh, this is a hopeless country! There's a fellow that thinks that the four cardinal virtues are not to be found outside an Irish Republic. I don't want to boast about myself—I don't want to boast about myself, and I suppose I could call meself as good a Gael as some of those that are knocking about now—knocking about now—as good a Gael as some that are knocking about now,—but I remember the

125

time when I taught Irish six nights a week, when in the Irish Republican Brotherhood I payed me rifle levy like a man, an' when the Church refused to have anything to do with James Stephens, I tarred a prayer for the repose of his soul on the steps of the Pro-Cathedral. Now, after all me work for Dark Rosaleen, the only answer you can get from a roarin' Republican to a simple question is " good-by . . . ee ". What, in the name o' God, can be bringin' him to Knocksedan?

DAVOREN. Hadn't you better run out and ask him?

SEUMAS. That's right, that's right—make a joke about it! That's the Irish People all over—they treat a joke as a serious thing and a serious thing as a joke. Upon me soul, I'm beginning to believe that the Irish People aren't, never were an' never will be fit for self-government. They've made Balor of the Evil Eye King of Ireland, an' so signs on it there's neither conscience nor honesty from one end of the country to the other. Well, I hope he'll have a happy day in Knocksedan. (*A knock at the door.*) Who's that? (*Another knock.*)

SEUMAS (*irritably*). Who's that; who's there?
DAVOREN (*more irritably*). Halt and give the

countersign—damn it, man, can't you go and see?

> (SEUMAS *goes over and opens the door. A man of about sixty is revealed, dressed in a faded blue serge suit; a half tall hat is on his head. It is evident that he has no love for* SEUMAS, *who denies him the deference he believes is due from a tenant to a landlord. He carries some papers in his hand.*)

THE LANDLORD (*ironically*). Good-day, Mr. Shields; it's meself that hopes you're feelin' well—you're lookin' well, anyhow—though you can't always go be looks nowadays.

SEUMAS. It doesn't matter whether I'm looking well or feelin' well; I'm all right, thanks be to God.

THE LANDLORD. I'm very glad to hear it.

SEUMAS. It doesn't matter whether you're glad to hear it or not, Mr. Mulligan.

THE LANDLORD. You're not inclined to be very civil, Mr. Shields.

SEUMAS. Look here, Mr. Mulligan, if you come here to raise an argument, I've something to do—let me tell you that.

THE LANDLORD. I don't come here to raise no argument; a person ud have small gains argufyin' with you—let me tell you that.

SEUMAS. I've no time to be standin' here gostherin' with you—let me shut the door, Mr. Mulligan.

THE LANDLORD. You'll not shut no door till you've heard what I've got to say.

SEUMAS. Well, say it then, an' go about your business.

THE LANDLORD. You're very high an' mighty, but take care you're not goin' to get a drop. What a baby you are not to know what brings me here. Maybe you thought I was goin' to ask you to come to tea.

DAVOREN. Ah me! alas, pain, pain ever, for ever!

SEUMAS. Are you goin' to let me shut the door, Mr. Mulligan?

THE LANDLORD. I'm here for me rent; you don't like the idea of bein' asked to pay your just an' lawful debts.

SEUMAS. You'll get your rent when you learn to keep your rent-book in a proper way.

THE LANDLORD. I'm not goin' to take any lessons from you, anyhow.

SEUMAS. I want to have no more talk with you, Mr. Mulligan.

THE LANDLORD. Talk or no talk, you owe me eleven weeks' rent, an' it's marked down again' you in black an' white.

SEUMAS. I don't care a damn if it was marked down in green, white an' yellow.

THE LANDLORD. You're a terribly independent fellow, an' it ud be fitter for you to be less funny an' stop tryin' to be billickin' honest an' respectable people.

SEUMAS. Just you be careful what you're sayin', Mr. Mulligan. There's law in the land still.

THE LANDLORD. Be me sowl there is, an' you're goin' to get a little of it now. (*He offers the papers to* SEUMAS) Them's for you.

SEUMAS (*hesitating to take them*). I want to have nothing to do with you, Mr. Mulligan.

THE LANDLORD (*throwing the papers in the centre of the room*). What am I better? It was the sorry day I ever let you come into this house. Maybe them notices to quit will stop your writin' letters to the papers about me an' me house.

DAVOREN. For goodness' sake, bring the man in, and don't be discussing the situation like a pair of primitive troglodytes.

SEUMAS (*taking no notice*). Writing letters to the papers is my business, an' I'll write as often as I like, when I like an' how I like.

THE LANDLORD. You'll not write about this house at all events. You can blow about the

state of the yard, but you took care to say
nothin' about payin' rent: oh no, that's not in
your line.   But since you're not satisfied with
the house you can pack up an' go to another.

SEUMAS. I'll go, Mr. Mulligan, when I
think fit, an' no sooner.

THE LANDLORD. Not content with keeping
the rent, you're startin' to bring in lodgers—
(*to* DAVOREN) not that I'm sayin' anythin'
again' you, sir.   Bringin' in lodgers without
as much as be your leave—what's the world
comin' to at all that a man's house isn't his own?
But I'll soon put a stop to your gallop, for on the
twenty-eight of the next month out you go,
an' there'll be few sorry to see your back.

SEUMAS. I'll go when I like.

THE LANDLORD. I'll let you see whether you
own the house or no.

SEUMAS. I'll go when I like!

THE LANDLORD. We'll see about that.

SEUMAS. We'll see.

THE LANDLORD. Ay, we'll see.

> (THE LANDLORD *goes out and* SEUMAS
> *shuts the door.*)

THE LANDLORD (*outside*).   Mind you, I'm
in earnest; you'll not stop in this house a
minute longer than the twenty-eight.

SEUMAS (*with a roar*). Ah, go to hell!

DAVOREN (*pacing the room as far as the space will permit*). What in the name of God persuaded me to come to such a house as this?

SEUMAS. It's nothing when you're used to it; you're too thin-skinned altogether. The oul' sod's got the wind up about you, that's all.

DAVOREN. Got the wind up about me!

SEUMAS. He thinks you're on the run. He's afraid of a raid, and that his lovely property'll be destroyed.

DAVOREN. But why, in the name of all that's sensible, should he think that I'm on the run?

SEUMAS. Sure they all think you're on the run. Mrs. Henderson thinks it, Tommy Owens thinks it, Mrs. an' Mr. Grigson think it, an' Minnie Powell thinks it too. (*Picking up his attaché case*) I'd better be off if I'm goin' to do anything to-day.

DAVOREN. What are we going to do with these notices to quit?

SEUMAS. Oh, shove them up on the mantelpiece behind one of the statues.

DAVOREN. Oh, I mean what action shall we take?

SEUMAS. I haven't time to stop now. We'll talk about them when I come back. . . . I'll get me own back on that oul' Mulligan yet. I wish to God they would come an' smash his rookery to pieces, for it's all he thinks of, and, mind you, oul' Mulligan would call himself a descendant of the true Gaels of Banba—(*as he goes out*):

> Oh, proud were the chieftains of famed Inisfail.
> Is truagh gan oidher 'na Vfarradh.
> The stars of our sky an' the salt of our soil—

Oh, Kathleen ni Houlihan, your way's a thorny way!

(*He goes out.*)

DAVOREN (*returning to the table and sitting down at the typewriter*). Oh, Donal Og O'Davoren, your way's a thorny way. Your last state is worse than your first. Ah me, alas! Pain, pain ever, for ever. Like thee, Prometheus, no change, no pause, no hope. Ah, life, life, life! (*There is a gentle knock at the door.*) Another Fury come to plague me now!

(*Another knock, a little louder.*)

DAVOREN. You can knock till you're tired.

(*The door opens and* MINNIE POWELL *enters with an easy confidence one would not expect her to possess from her gentle way of knocking. She is a girl of twenty-three, but the fact of being forced to earn her living, and to take care of herself, on account of her parents' early death, has given her a force and an*

*assurance beyond her years. She has
lost the sense of fear (she does not know
this), and, consequently, she is at ease
in all places and before all persons,
even those of a superior education, so
long as she meets them in the atmosphere
that surrounds the members of her own
class. Her hair is brown, neither light
nor dark, but partaking of both tints
according to the light or shade she may
happen to be in. Her well-shaped
figure—a rare thing in a city girl—
is charmingly dressed in a brown tailor-
made costume, her stockings and shoes
are a darker brown tint than the
costume, and all are crowned by a silk
tam-o'-shanter of a rich blue tint.)*

MINNIE. Are you in, Mr. Shields?

DAVOREN (*rapidly*). No, he's not, Minnie;
he's just gone out—if you run out quickly
you're sure to catch him.

MINNIE. Oh, it's all right, Mr. Davoren,
you'll do just as well; I just come in for a drop
o' milk for a cup o' tea; I shouldn't be troublin'
you this way, but I'm sure you don't mind.

DAVOREN (*dubiously*). No trouble in the
world; delighted, I'm sure. (*Giving her the
milk*) There, will you have enough?

MINNIE. Plenty, lashins, thanks. Do you be all alone all the day, Mr. Davoren?

DAVOREN. No, indeed; I wish to God I was.

MINNIE. It's not good for you then. I don't know how you like to be by yourself—I couldn't stick it long.

DAVOREN (*wearily*). No?

MINNIE. No, indeed; (*with rapture*) there's nothin' I'm more fond of than a Hooley. I was at one last Sunday—I danced rings round me! Tommy Owens was there—you know Tommy Owens, don't you?

DAVOREN. I can't say I do.

MINNIE. D'ye not? The little fellow that lives with his mother in the two-pair back—(*ecstatically*) he's a gorgeous melodeon player!

DAVOREN. A gifted son of Orpheus, eh?

MINNIE (*who never heard of Orpheus*). You've said it, Mr. Davoren: the son of poor oul' Battie Owens, a weeshy, dawny, bit of a man that was never sober an' was always talkin' politics. Poor man, it killed him in the long run.

DAVOREN. A man should always be drunk, Minnie, when he talks politics—it's the only way in which to make them important.

MINNIE. Tommy takes after the oul' fellow, too; he'd talk from morning till night when he has a few jars in him. (*Suddenly; for like all of her class,* MINNIE *is not able to converse very long on the one subject, and her thoughts spring from one thing to another*) Poetry is a grand thing, Mr. Davoren, I'd love to be able to write a poem—a lovely poem on Ireland an' the men o' '98.

DAVOREN. Oh, we've had enough of poems, Minnie, about '98, and of Ireland, too.

MINNIE. Oh, there's a thing for a Republican to say!   But I know what you mean : it's time to give up the writing an' take to the gun. (*Her roving eye catches sight of the flowers in the vase*) What's Mr. Shields doin' with the oul' weeds?

DAVOREN. Those aren't Shields', they're mine.   Wild flowers is a kindlier name for them, Minnie, than weeds.   These are wild violets, this is an *Arum maculatum*, or Wake Robin, and these are Celandines, a very beautiful flower related to the buttercups. (*He quotes*):

> One day, when Morn's half-open'd eyes
> Were bright with Spring sunshine—
> My hand was clasp'd in yours, dear love,
> And yours was clasp'd in mine—
> We bow'd as worshippers before
> The Golden Celandine.

MINNIE. Oh, aren't they lovely, an' isn't the poem lovely, too! I wonder, now, who she was.

DAVOREN (*puzzled*). She, who?

MINNIE. Why the . . . (*roguishly*) Oh, be the way you don't know.

DAVOREN. Know? I'm sure I don't know.

MINNIE. It doesn't matter, anyhow—that's your own business; I suppose I don't know her.

DAVOREN. Know her, know whom?

MINNIE (*shyly*). Her whose hand was clasped in yours, an' yours was clasped in hers.

DAVOREN. Oh that—that was simply a poem I quoted about the Celandine, that might apply to any girl—to you, for instance.

MINNIE (*greatly relieved, coming over and sitting beside* DAVOREN). But you have a sweetheart, all the same, Mr. Davoren, haven't you?

DAVOREN. I? No, not one, Minnie.

MINNIE. Oh, now, you can tell that to some one else; aren't you a poet an' aren't all the girls fond o' poets?

DAVOREN. That may be, but all the poets aren't fond of girls.

MINNIE. They are in the story-books, ay, and fond of more than one, too. (*With a questioning look*) Are you fond of them, Mr. Davoren?

DAVOREN. Of course I like girls, Minnie, especially girls who can add to their charms by the way in which they dress, like you, for instance.

MINNIE. Oh, now, you're on for coddin' me, Mr. Davoren.

DAVOREN. No, really, Minnie, I'm not; you are a very charming little girl indeed.

MINNIE. Then if I'm a charmin' little girl, you ought to be able to write a poem about me.

DAVOREN (*who has become susceptible to the attractiveness of* MINNIE, *catching her hand*). And so I will, so I will, Minnie; I have written them about girls not half so pretty as yourself.

MINNIE. Ah, I knew you had one, I knew you had one now.

DAVOREN. Nonsense. Every girl a poet writes about isn't his sweetheart; Annie Laurie wasn't the sweetheart of Bobbie Burns.

MINNIE. You needn't tell me she wasn't; " An' for bonnie Annie Laurie I'd lay me down an' die." No man ud lay down an' die for any but a sweetheart, not even for a wife.

DAVOREN. No man, Minnie, willingly dies for anything.

137

MINNIE. Except for his country, like Robert Emmet.

DAVOREN. Even he would have lived on if he could; he died not to deliver Ireland. The British Government killed him to save the British nation.

MINNIE. You're only jokin' now; you'd die for your country.

DAVOREN. I don't know so much about that.

MINNIE. You would, you would, you would —I know what you are.

DAVOREN. What am I?

MINNIE (*in a whisper*). A gunman on the run!

DAVOREN (*too pleased to deny it*). Maybe I am, and maybe I'm not.

MINNIE. Oh, I know, I know, I know. Do you never be afraid?

DAVOREN. Afraid!   Afraid of what?

MINNIE. Why, the ambushes of course; *I'm* all of a tremble when I hear a shot go off, an' what must it be to be in the middle of the firin'?

DAVOREN (*delighted at* MINNIE'S *obvious admiration; leaning back in his chair, and lighting a cigarette with placid affectation*). I'll admit one does be a little nervous at first, but a fellow gets used to it after a bit, till, at last, a gunman throws a bomb as carelessly as a schoolboy throws a snowball.

MINNIE (*fervently*). I wish it was all over, all the same. (*Suddenly, with a tremor in her voice*) You'll take care of yourself, won't you, won't you, Donal—I mean, Mr. Davoren?

DAVOREN (*earnestly*). Call me Donal, Minnie; we're friends, great friends now—(*putting his arm around her*) Go on, Minnie, call me Donal, let me hear you say Donal.

MINNIE. The place badly needs a tidyin' up . . . Donal—there now, are you satisfied? (*Rapidly, half afraid of* DAVOREN's *excited emotions*) But it really does, it's in an awful state. To-morrow's a half-day, an' I'll run in an' straighten it up a bit.

DAVOREN (*frightened at the suggestion*). No, no, Minnie, you're too pretty for that sort of work; besides, the people of the house would be sure to start talking about you.

MINNIE. An' do you think Minnie Powell cares whether they'll talk or no? I've had to push me way through life up to this without help from any one, an' she's not goin' to ask their leave, now, to do what she wants to do.

DAVOREN (*forgetting his timidity in the honest joy of appreciating the independent courage of*

139

MINNIE). My soul within art thou, Minnie!
A pioneer in action as I am a pioneer in thought.
The two powers that shall " grasp this sorry
scheme of things entire, and mould life nearer
to the heart's desire ".   Lovely little Minnie,
and brave as well; brave little Minnie, and
lovely as well!

> (*His disengaged hand lifts up her bent
> head, and he looks earnestly at her; he
> is stooping to kiss her when* TOMMY
> OWENS *appears at the door, which*
> MINNIE *has left partially open.* TOMMY
> *is about twenty-five years of age.   He
> is small and thin; his words are
> uttered in a nasal drawl; his voice is
> husky, due to frequent drinks and per-
> petual cigarette-smoking.   He tries to
> get rid of the huskiness by an occasional
> cough.*   TOMMY *is a hero-worshipper,
> and, like many others, he is anxious to
> be on familiar terms with those whom
> he thinks are braver than he is himself,
> and whose approbation he tries to win
> by an assumption equal to their own.
> He talks in a staccato manner.   He has
> a few drinks taken—it is too early to
> be drunk—that make him talkative.
> He is dressed in a suit of dongarees,*

and gives a gentle cough to draw atten-
tion to his presence.)

TOMMY. I seen nothin'—honest—thought
you was learnin' to typewrite—Mr. Davoren
teachin' you.   I seen nothin' else—s'help me
God!

MINNIE. We'd be hard put to it if we
minded what you seen, Tommy Owens.

TOMMY. Right, Minnie, Tommy Owens
has a heart—Evenin', Mr. Davoren—don't
mind me comin' in — I'm Tommy Owens
—live up in the two-pair back, workin' in
Ross an' Walpole's — Mr. Shields knows
me well; you needn't be afraid o' me, Mr.
Davoren.

DAVOREN. Why should I be afraid of you,
Mr. Owens, or of anybody else?

TOMMY. Why should you, indeed?   We're
all friends here—Mr. Shields knows me well—
all you've got to say is, "Do you know Tommy
Owens?" an' he'll tell you the sort of a man
Tommy Owens is.   There's no flies on Tommy
—got me?

MINNIE. For goodness' sake, Tommy, leave
Mr. Davoren alone—he's got enough burgeons
on him already.

TOMMY. Not a word, Minnie, not a word—
Mr. Davoren understands me well, as man to

man. It's "Up the Republic" all the time—eh, Mr. Davoren?

DAVOREN. I know nothing about the Republic; I have no connection with the politics of the day, and I don't want to have any connection.

TOMMY. You needn't say no more—a nod's as good as a wink to a blind horse—you've no meddlin' or makin' with it good, bad, or indifferent, pro nor con; I know it an' Minnie knows it—give me your hand. (*He catches* DAVOREN's *hand*.) Two firm hands clasped together will all the power outbrave of the heartless English tyrant, the Saxon coward an' knave. That's Tommy Owens' hand, Mr. Davoren, the hand of a man, a man— Mr. Shields knows me well. (*He breaks into song.*)

High upon the gallows tree stood the noble-hearted three,
By the vengeful tyrant stricken in their bloom;
But they met him face to face with the spirit of their race,
And they went with souls undaunted to their doom!

MINNIE (*in an effort to quell his fervour*). Tommy Owens, for goodness' sake . . .

TOMMY (*overwhelming her with a shout*):

God save Ireland ses the hayros, God save Ireland ses
    we all
Whether on the scaffold high or the battle-field we die,
Oh, what matter when for Ayryinn dear we fall!

(*Tearfully*) Mr. Davoren, I'd die for Ireland!

DAVOREN. I know you would, I know you
would, Tommy.

TOMMY. I never got a chance—they never
gave me a chance—but all the same I'd be
there if I was called on—Mr. Shields knows
that—ask Mr. Shields, Mr. Davoren.

DAVOREN. There's no necessity, Tommy;
I know you're the right stuff if you got the
chance, but remember that " he also serves
who only stands and waits ".

TOMMY (*fiercely*). I'm bloody well tired o'
waitin'—we're all tired o' waitin'. Why isn't
every man in Ireland out with the I.R.A.?
Up with the barricades, up with the barricades;
it's now or never, now an' for ever, as Sarsfield
said at the battle o' Vinegar Hill. Up with
the barricades—that's Tommy Owens—an' a
penny buys a whistle. Let them as thinks
different say different—what do you say,
Mr. Davoren?

DAVOREN. I say, Tommy, you ought to go
up and get your dinner, for if you wait much
longer it won't be worth eating.

TOMMY. Oh, damn the dinner; who'd think o' dinner an' Ireland fightin' to be free —not Tommy Owens, anyhow. It's only the Englishman who's always thinkin' of his belly.

MINNIE. Tommy Owens!

TOMMY. Excuse me, Miss Powell, in the ardure ov me anger I disremembered there was a lady present.

> (*Voices are heard outside, and presently* MRS. HENDERSON *comes into the room, followed by* MR. GALLOGHER, *who, however, lingers at the door, too timid to come any farther.* MRS. HENDERSON *is a massive woman in every way; massive head, arms and body; massive voice, and a massive amount of self-confidence. She is a mountain of good nature, and during the interview she behaves towards* DAVOREN *with deferential self-assurance. She dominates the room, and seems to occupy the whole of it. She is dressed poorly, but tidily, wearing a white apron and a large shawl.* MR. GALLOGHER, *on the other hand, is a spare little man with a spare little grey beard, and a thin, nervous voice. He is dressed as well as a faded suit of blue will allow him to be.*

*He is obviously ill at ease during his
interview with* DAVOREN. *He carries
a hard hat, much the worse for wear,
under his left arm, and a letter in his
right hand.*)

MRS. HENDERSON (*entering the room*). Come
along in, Mr. Gallicker, Mr. Davoren won't
mind; it's him as can put you in the way o'
havin' your wrongs righted; come on in, man,
an' don't be so shy—Mr. Davoren is wan ov
ourselves that stands for govermint ov the
people with the people by the people.   You'll
find you'll be as welcome as the flowers in May.
Good evenin', Mr. Davoren, an' God an' His
holy angels be between you an' all harm.

TOMMY (*effusively*). Come on, Mr. Gallicker,
an' don't be a stranger—we're all friends here
—anything special to be done or particular
advice asked, here's your man here.

DAVOREN (*subconsciously pleased, but a little
timid of the belief that he is connected with the
gunmen*). I'm very busy just now, Mrs. Henderson, and really . . .

MRS. HENDERSON (*mistaking the reason of his
embarrassment*). Don't be put out, Mr. Davoren,
we won't keep you more nor a few minutes.
It's not in me or in Mr. Gallicker to spoil sport.
Him an' me was young once, an' knows what

it is to be strolling at night in the pale moon-light, with arms round one another. An' I wouldn't take much an' say there's game in Mr. Gallicker still, for I seen, sometimes, a dangerous cock in his eye. But we won't keep you an' Minnie long asunder; he's the letter an' all written. You must know, Mr. Davoren—excuse me for not introducin' him sooner—this is Mr. Gallicker, that lives in the front drawin'-room ov number fifty-five, as decent an' honest an' quiet a man as you'd meet in a day's walk. An' so signs on it, it's them as 'ill be imposed upon—read the letter, Mr. Gallicker.

TOMMY. Read away, Mr. Gallicker, it will be attended to, never fear; we know our own know, eh, Mr. Davoren?

MINNIE. Hurry up, Mr. Gallicker, an' don't be keeping Mr. Davoren.

MRS. HENDERSON. Give him time, Minnie Powell. Give him time. You must know in all fairity, Mr. Davoren, that the family livin' in the next room to Mr. Gallicker—the back drawin'-room, to be particular—am I right or am I wrong, Mr. Gallicker?

MR. GALLOGHER. You're right, Mrs. Henderson, perfectly right, indeed—that's the very identical room.

146

MRS. HENDERSON. Well, Mr. Davoren, the people in the back drawin'-room, or, to be more particular, the residents—that's the word that's writ in the letter—am I right or am I wrong, Mr. Gallicker?

MR. GALLOGHER. You're right, Mrs. Henderson, perfectly accurate—that's the very identical word.

MRS. HENDERSON. Well, Mr. Davoren, the residents in the back drawin'-room, as I aforesaid, is nothin' but a gang o' tramps that oughtn't to be allowed to associate with honest, decent, quiet, respectable people. Mr. Gallicker has tried to reason with them, and make them behave themselves—which in my opinion they never will—however, that's only an opinion, an' not legal—ever since they have made Mr. Gallicker's life a HELL! Mr Gallicker, am I right or am I wrong?

MR. GALLOGHER. I'm sorry to say you're right, Mrs. Henderson, perfectly right—not a word of exaggeration.

MRS. HENDERSON. Well, now, Mr. Gallicker, seein' as I have given Mr. Davoren a fair account of how you're situated, an' of these tramps' cleverality, I'll ask you to read the letter, which I'll say, not because you're there, or that you're a friend o' mine, is as good a letter as was decomposed by a scholar.   Now, Mr. Gallicker, an' don't forget the top sayin'.

> (MR. GALLOGHER *prepares to read;* MINNIE *leans forward to listen;* TOMMY *takes out a well-worn note-book and a pencil stump, and assumes a very important attitude.*)

TOMMY. One second. Mr. Gallicker, is this the twenty-first or twenty-second?

MR. GALLOGHER. The twenty-first, sir.

TOMMY. Thanks; proceed, Mr. Gallicker.

MR. GALLOGHER (*with a few preliminary tremors, reads the letter*).
(*Reading*):

> TO ALL TO WHOM THESE PRESENTS COME, GREETING
> Gentlemen of the Irish Republican Army . .

MRS. HENDERSON. There's a beginnin' for you, Mr. Davoren.

MINNIE. That's some swank.

TOMMY. There's a lot in that sayin', mind you; it's a hard wallop at the British Empire.

MRS. HENDERSON (*proudly*). Go on, Mr. Gallicker.

MR. GALLOGHER (*reading*):

> " I wish to call your attention to the persecution me and my family has to put up with in respect of and

appertaining to the residents of the back drawing-room of the house known as fifty-five, Saint Teresa Street, situate in the Parish of St. Thomas, in the Borough and City of Dublin.   This persecution started eighteen months ago—or to be precise—on the tenth day of the sixth month, in the year nineteen hundred and twenty."

MRS. HENDERSON. That's the word I was trying to think ov—precise—it cuts the ground from under their feet—so to speak.

MR. GALLOGHER (*reading*):

" We, the complainants, resident on the ground floor, deeming it disrespectable . . ."

MRS. HENDERSON (*with an emphatic nod*). Which it was.

MR. GALLOGHER (*reading*):

" Deeming it disrespectable to have an open hall door, and to have the hall turned into a playground, made a solemn protest, and, in consequence, we the complainants aforesaid has had no peace ever since. Owing to the persecution, as aforesaid specified, we had to take out a summons again them some time ago as there was no Republican Courts then; but we did not proceed again them as me and my wife—to wit, James and Winifred Gallogher—has a strong objection to foreign Courts as such.   We had peace for some time after that, but now things have gone from bad to worse.   The name calling and the language is something abominable. . . ."

149

MRS. HENDERSON (*holding out her hand as a constable would extend his to stop a car that another may pass*). Excuse me, Mr. Gallicker, but I think the word " shockin' " should be put in there after abominable; for the language used be these tramps has two ways o' bein' looked at—for it's abominable to the childer an' shockin' to your wife—am I right or am I wrong, Mr. Davoren?

TOMMY (*judicially*). Shockin' is a right good word, with a great deal o' meanin', an' . . .

MRS. HENDERSON (*with a deprecating gesture that extinguishes* TOMMY). Tommy, let Mr. Davoren speak; whatever Mr. Davoren ses, Julia Henderson'll abide be.

DAVOREN (*afraid to say anything else*). I think the word might certainly be introduced with advantage.

MRS. HENDERSON. Go over there, Mr. Gallicker, an' put in the word shockin', as aforesaid.

(GALLOGHER *goes over to the table, and with a great deal of difficulty enters the word.*)

TOMMY (*to* MR. GALLOGHER *as he writes*). Ey, there's two k's in shockin'!

MR. GALLOGHER (*reading*):

" The language is something abominable and shocking.   My wife has often to lock the door of the room to keep them from assaulting her.   If you would be so kind as to send some of your army or police down to see for themselves we would give them full particulars.   I have to be always from home all day, as I work with Mr. Hennessy, the harness maker of the Coombe, who will furnish all particulars as to my unvarnished respectability, also my neighbours.   The name of the resident-tenant who is giving all this trouble and who, pursuant to the facts of the case aforesaid, mentioned, will be the defendant, is Dwyer. The husband of the aforesaid Mrs. Dwyer, or the aforesaid defendant, as the case may be, is a seaman, who is coming home shortly, and we beg The Irish Republican Army to note that the said Mrs. Dwyer says he will settle us when he comes home.   While leaving it entirely in the hands of the gentlemen of The Republican Army, the defendant, that is to say, James Gallogher of fifty-five St. Teresa Street, ventures to say that he thinks he has made out a Primmy Fashy Case against Mrs. Dwyer and all her heirs, male and female as aforesaid mentioned in the above written schedule.

" *N.B.*—If you send up any of your men, please tell them to bring their guns.   I beg to remain the humble servant and devoted admirer of the Gentlemen of the Irish Republican Army.

" Witness my hand this tenth day of the fifth month of the year nineteen hundred and twenty.

" JAMES GALLOGHER."

MR. GALLOGHER (*with a modest cough*). Ahem.

MRS. HENDERSON. There's a letter for you, Mr. Davoren!

TOMMY. It's the most powerfullest letter I ever heard read.

MINNIE. It wasn't you, really, that writ it, Mr. Gallicker?

MRS. HENDERSON. Sinn Fein Amhain: him an' him only, Minnie. I seen him with me own two eyes when me an' Winnie—Mrs. Gallicker, Mr. Davoren, aforesaid as appears in the letter—was havin' a chat be the fire.

MINNIE. You'd never think it was in him to do it.

MRS. HENDERSON. An' to think that the likes ov such a man is to have the sowl-case worried out ov him by a gang o' tramps; but it's in good hands now, an' instead ov them settlin' yous, Mr. Gallicker, it's yous 'ill settle them. Give the letter to Mr. Davoren, an' we'll be goin'.

(GALLOGHER *gives the letter to* DAVOREN.)

MRS. HENDERSON (*moving towards the door*). I hope you an' Mr. Shields is gettin' on all right together, Mr. Davoren.

DAVOREN. Fairly well, thanks, Mrs. Henderson. We don't see much of each other. He's out during the day, and I'm usually out during the evening.

152

MRS. HENDERSON. I'm afraid he'll never make a fortune out ov what he's sellin'. He'll talk above an hour over a pennorth o' pins. Every time he comes to our place I buy a package o' hairpins from him to give him a little encouragement. I 'clare to God I have as many pins now as ud make a wire mattress for a double bed. All the young divils about the place are beginnin' to make a jeer ov him, too; I gave one ov them a mallavogin' the other day for callin' him oul' hairpins!

MR. GALLOGHER (*venturing an opinion*). Mr. Shields is a man of exceptional mental capacity, and is worthy of a more dignified position.

MRS. HENDERSON. Them words is true, Mr. Gallicker, and they aren't. For to be wise is to be a fool, an' to be a fool is to be wise.

MR. GALLOGHER (*with deprecating tolerance*). Oh, Mrs. Henderson, that's a parrotox.

MRS. HENDERSON. It may be what a parrot talks, or a blackbird, or, for the matter of that, a lark—but it's what Julia Henderson thinks, any . . . whisht, is that a *Stop Press*?

(*Outside is heard the shriek of a newsboy calling " Stop Press ".*)

MRS. HENDERSON. Run out, Tommy, an' get it till we see what it is.

TOMMY. I haven't got a make.

153

MRS. HENDERSON. I never seen you any other way, an' you'll be always the same if you keep follyin' your Spearmints, an' your Bumble Bees an' your Night Patrols. (*Shouting to some one outside*) Is that a *Stop Press*, Mrs. Grigson?

VOICE OUTSIDE. Yis; an ambush out near Knocksedan.

MRS. HENDERSON. That's the stuff to give them. (*Loudly*) Was there anybody hurted?

VOICE OUTSIDE. One poor man killed—some chap named Maguire, the paper says.

DAVOREN (*agitated*). What name did she say?

MINNIE. Maguire; did you know him, Mr. Davoren?

DAVOREN. Yes—no, no; I didn't know him, no, I didn't know him, Minnie.

MINNIE. I wonder is it the Maguire that does be with Mr. Shields?

DAVOREN. Oh no, not at all, it couldn't be.

MRS. HENDERSON. Knocksedan? That's in the County Sligo, now, or I'm greatly mistaken —am I right, Mr. Gallicker, or am I wrong?

MR. GALLOGHER (*who knows perfectly well that it is in the County Dublin, but dare not correct* MRS. HENDERSON). That's where it is—Knocksedan, that's the very identical county.

154

MRS. HENDERSON. Well, I think we better be makin' a move, Mr. Gallicker; we've kep Mr. Davoren long enough, an' you'll find the letter 'll be in good hans.

> (MR. GALLOGHER *and* MRS. HENDERSON *move towards the door, which when he reaches it* MR. GALLOGHER *grips, hesitates, turns and buttoning his coat, says*):

Mr. Davoren, sir, on behalf ov meself, James Gallicker, an' Winifred, Mrs. Gallicker, wife ov the said James, I beg to offer, extend an' furnish our humble an' hearty thanks for your benevolent goodness in interferin' in the matter specified, particularated an' expanded upon in the letter, mandamus or schedule, as the case may be. An' let me interpretate to you on behalf ov meself an' Winifred Gallicker, that whenever you visit us you will be supernally positive of a hundred thousand welcomes— ahem.

MRS. HENDERSON (*beaming with pride for the genius of her friend*). There's a man for you, Mr. Davoren! You forgot to mention Biddy and Shaun, Mr. Gallicker—(*to* DAVOREN) his two children—it's himself has them trained well. It ud make your heart thrill like an alarm clock to hear them singin' " Faith ov Our

Fathers " an' " Wrap the Green Flag Roun'
Me."

MR. GALLOGHER (*half apologetically and half
proudly*). Faith an' Fatherland, Mrs. Henderson, Faith and Fatherland.

MRS. HENDERSON. Well, good-day, Mr.
Davoren, an' God keep you an' strengthen all
the men that are fightin' for Ireland's freedom.
(*She and* GALLOGHER *go out*.)

TOMMY. I must be off too, so long, Mr.
Davoren, an' remember that Tommy Owens
only waits the call. (*He goes out too*.)

DAVOREN. Well, Minnie, we're by ourselves once more.

MINNIE. Wouldn't that Tommy Owens give
you the sick—only waitin' to hear the call!
Ah, then it'll take all the brass bands in the
country to blow the call before Tommy Owens
ud hear it. (*She looks at her wristlet watch*.)
Sacred Heart, I've only ten minutes to get
back to work! I'll have to fly! Quick, Mr.
Davoren, write me name in typewritin' before
I go—just " Minnie ".
(DAVOREN *types the name*.)

MINNIE (*shyly but determinedly*). Now yours
underneath—just " Donal ". (DAVOREN *does
so*.) Minnie, Donal; Donal, Minnie; good-
bye now.

156

DAVOREN. Here, what about your milk?

MINNIE. I haven't time to take it now. (*Slyly*) I'll come for it this evening.

(*They both go towards the door.*)

DAVOREN. Minnie, the kiss I didn't get.

MINNIE. What kiss?

DAVOREN. When we were interrupted; you know, you little rogue, come, just one.

MINNIE. Quick, then.

(DAVOREN *kisses her and she runs out.*)
(DAVOREN *returns thoughtfully to the table.*)

DAVOREN. Minnie, Donal; Donal, Minnie. Very pretty, but very ignorant. A Gunman on the run! Be careful, be careful, Donal Davoren. But Minnie is attracted to the idea, and I am attracted to Minnie. And what danger can there be in being the shadow of a gunman?

CURTAIN

ACT II

Scene: *The same as in Act I. But it is now night.* SEUMAS *is in the bed that runs along the wall at back.* DAVOREN *is seated near the fire, to which he has drawn the table. He has a fountain-pen in his hand, and is attracted in thought towards the Moon, which is shining in through the windows. An open writing-pad is on the table at* DAVOREN'S *elbow. The bag left by* MAGUIRE *is still in the same place.*

DAVOREN:

The cold chaste moon, the Queen of Heaven's bright
  isles,
Who makes all beautiful on which she smiles;
That wandering shrine of soft yet icy flame,
Which ever is transformed yet still the same.

Ah, Shelley, Shelley, you yourself were a
lovely human orb shining through clouds of

whirling human dust. " She makes all beautiful on which she smiles." Ah, Shelley, she couldn't make this thrice accursed room beautiful. Her beams of beauty only make its horrors more full of horrors still. There is an ugliness that can be made beautiful, and there is an ugliness that can only be destroyed, and this is part of that ugliness. Donal, Donal, I fear your last state is worse than your first.

> (*He lilts a verse, which he writes in the pad before him.*)

When night advances through the sky with slow
    And solemn tread,
The queenly moon looks down on life below,
    As if she read
Man's soul, and in her scornful silence said :
    All beautiful and happiest things are dead.

SEUMAS (*sleepily*). Donal, Donal, are you awake? (*A pause.*) Donal, Donal, are you asleep?

DAVOREN. I'm neither awake nor asleep: I'm thinking.

SEUMAS. I was just thinkin', too—I was just thinkin', too, that Maguire is sorry now that he didn't come with me instead of going to Knocksedan. He caught something besides butterflies—two of them he got, one through each lung.

DAVOREN. The Irish people are very fond of turning a serious thing into a joke; that was a serious affair—for poor Maguire.

SEUMAS (*defensively*). Why didn't he do what he arranged to do? Did he think of me when he was goin' to Knocksedan? How can he expect me to have any sympathy with him now?

DAVOREN. He can hardly expect that now that he's dead.

SEUMAS. The Republicans 'll do a lot for him, now. How am I goin' to get back the things he has belongin' to me, either? There's some of them in that bag over there, but that's not quarter of what he had; an' I don't know where he was stoppin', for he left his old digs a week or so ago—I suppose there's nothing to be said about my loss; I'm to sing dumb.

DAVOREN. I hope there's nothing else in the bag, besides thread and hairpins.

SEUMAS. What else ud be in it? . . . I can't sleep properly ever since they put on this damned curfew. A minute ago I thought I heard some of the oul' ones standin' at the door; they won't be satisfied till they bring a raid on the house; an' they never begin to stand at the door till after curfew. . . . Are you gone to bed, Donal?

DAVOREN. No; I'm trying to finish this poem.

SEUMAS (*sitting up in bed*). If I was you I'd give that game up; it doesn't pay a working man to write poetry. I don't profess to know much about poetry—I don't profess to know much about poetry—about poetry—I don't know much about the pearly glint of the morning dew, or the damask sweetness of the rare wild rose, or the subtle greenness of the serpent's eye—but I think a poet's claim to greatness depends upon his power to put passion in the common people.

DAVOREN. Ay, passion to howl for his destruction. The People! Damn the people! They live in the abyss, the poet lives on the mountain-top; to the people there is no mystery of colour: it is simply the scarlet coat of the soldier; the purple vestments of a priest; the green banner of a party; the brown or blue overalls of industry. To them the might of design is a three-roomed house or a capacious bed. To them beauty is for sale in a butcher's shop. To the people the end of life is the life created for them; to the poet the end of life is the life that he creates for himself; life has a stifling grip upon the people's throat—it is the poet's musician. The poet ever strives to save the people; the people ever strive to destroy the poet. The people view life through creeds, through customs and through necessities; the poet views creeds, customs and necessities through life. The people . . .

SEUMAS (*suddenly, and with a note of anxiety in his voice*). Whisht! What's that? Is that the tappin' again?

DAVOREN. Tappin'. What tappin'?

SEUMAS (*in an awed whisper*). This is the second night I heard that tappin'! I believe it bodes no good to me. There, do you hear it again—a quiet, steady, mysterious tappin' on the wall.

DAVOREN. I hear no tappin'.

SEUMAS. It ud be better for me if you did. It's a sure sign of death when nobody hears it but meself.

DAVOREN. Death! What the devil are you talking about, man?

SEUMAS. I don't like it at all; there's always something like that heard when one of our family dies.

DAVOREN. I don't know about that; but I know there's a hell of a lot of things heard when one of your family lives.

SEUMAS. God between us an' all harm! Thank God I'm where I ought to be—in bed.

. . . It's always best to be in your proper place when such things happen — Sacred Heart! There it is again; do you not hear it now?

DAVOREN. Ah, for God's sake go asleep.

SEUMAS. Do you believe in nothing?

DAVOREN. I don't believe in tappin'.

SEUMAS. Whisht, it's stopped again; I'll try to go asleep for fear it ud begin again.

DAVOREN. Ay, do; and if it starts again I'll be sure to waken you up.

(*A pause.*)

SEUMAS. It's very cold to-night. Do you feel cold?

DAVOREN. I thought you were goin' asleep?

SEUMAS. The bloody cold won't let me. . . . You'd want a pair of pyjamas on you. (*A pause.*) Did you ever wear pyjamas, Donal?

DAVOREN. No, no, no.

SEUMAS. What kind of stuff is in them?

DAVOREN (*angrily*). Oh, it depends on the climate; in India, silk; in Italy, satin; and the Eskimo wears them made from the skin of the Polar bear.

SEUMAS (*emphatically*). If you take my advice you'll get into bed—that poem is beginnin' to get on your nerves.

DAVOREN (*extinguishing the candle with a*

163

vicious blow). Right; I'm going to bed now, so you can shut up.

    (Visibility is still maintained from the light of the moon.)

SEUMAS. I was goin' to say something when you put out the light—what's this it was— um, um, oh, ay: when I was comin' in this evenin' I saw Minnie Powell goin' out. If I was you I wouldn't have that one comin' in here.

DAVOREN. She comes in; I don't bring her in, do I?

SEUMAS. The oul' ones'll be talkin', an' once they start you don't know how it'll end. Surely a man that has read Shelley couldn't be interested in an ignorant little bitch that thinks of nothin' but jazz dances, fox trots, picture theatres an' dress.

DAVOREN. Right glad I am that she thinks of dress, for she thinks of it in the right way, and makes herself a pleasant picture to the eye. Education has been wasted on many persons, teaching them to talk only, but leaving with them all their primitive instincts. Had poor Minnie received an education she would have been an artist. She is certainly a pretty girl. I'm sure she is a good girl, and I believe she is a brave girl.

SEUMAS. A Helen of Troy come to live in a tenement! You think a lot about her simply because she thinks a lot about you, an' she thinks a lot about you because she looks upon you as a hero—a kind o' Paris . . . she'd give the world an' all to be gaddin' about with a gunman. An' what ecstasy it ud give her if after a bit you were shot or hanged; she'd be able to go about then—like a good many more—singin', " I do not mourn me darlin' lost, for he fell in his Jacket Green." An' then, for a year an' a day, all round her hat she'd wear the Tri-coloured Ribbon O, till she'd pick up an' marry some one else—possibly a British Tommy, with a Mons Star. An' as for bein' brave, it's easy to be that when you've no cause for cowardice; I wouldn't care to have me life dependin' on brave little Minnie Powell—she wouldn't sacrifice a jazz dance to save it.

DAVOREN (*sitting on the bed and taking off his coat and vest, preparatory to going to bed*). There; that's enough about Minnie Powell. I'm afraid I'll soon have to be on the run out of this house, too; it is becoming painfully obvious that there is no peace to be found here.

SEUMAS. Oh, this house is all right; barrin' the children, it does be quiet enough. Wasn't

165

there children in the last place you were in too?

DAVOREN. Ay, ten; (*viciously*) and they were all over forty.

> (*A pause as* DAVOREN *is removing his collar and tie.*)

SEUMAS. Everything is very quiet now; I wonder what time is it?

DAVOREN. The village cock hath thrice done salutation to the morn.

SEUMAS. Shakespeare, Richard the III., Act Five, Scene III. It was Ratcliffe said that to Richard just before the battle of Bosworth. . . . How peaceful the heavens look now with the moon in the middle; you'd never think there were men prowlin' about tryin' to shoot each other. I don't know how a man who has shot any one can sleep in peace at night.

DAVOREN. There's plenty of men can't sleep in peace at night now unless they know that they have shot somebody.

SEUMAS. I wish to God it was all over. The country is gone mad. Instead of counting their beads now they're countin' bullets; their Hail Marys and paternosters are burstin' bombs — burstin' bombs, an' the rattle of machine guns; petrol is their holy water; their Mass is a burnin' buildin'; their De

Profundis is " The Soldiers' Song ", an' their creed is, I believe in the gun almighty, maker of heaven an' earth—an' it's all for " the glory o' God an' the honour o' Ireland ".

DAVOREN. I remember the time when you yourself believed in nothing but the gun.

SEUMAS. Ay, when there wasn't a gun in the country; I've a different opinion now when there's nothin' but guns in the country. . . . An' you daren't open your mouth, for Kathleen Ni Houlihan is very different now to the woman who used to play the harp an' sing " Weep on, weep on, your hour is past ", for she's a ragin' divil now, an' if you only look crooked at her you're sure of a punch in th' eye.   But this is the way I look at it—I look at it this way: You're not goin'—you're not goin' to beat the British Empire—the British Empire, by shootin' an occasional Tommy at the corner of an occasional street.   Besides, when the Tommies have the wind up—when the Tommies have the wind up they let bang at everything they see —they don't give a God's curse who they plug.

DAVOREN. Maybe they ought to get down off the lorry and run to the Records Office to find out a man's pedigree before they plug him.

SEUMAS. It's the civilians that suffer; when there's an ambush they don't know where to run. Shot in the back to save the British Empire, an' shot in the breast to save the soul of Ireland. I'm a Nationalist meself, right enough—a Nationalist right enough, but all the same—I'm a Nationalist right enough; I believe in the freedom of Ireland, an' that England has no right to be here, but I draw the line when I hear the gunmen blowin' about dyin' for the people, when it's the people that are dyin' for the gunmen! With all due respect to the gunmen, I don't want them to die for me.

DAVOREN. Not likely; you object to any one of them deliberately dying for you for fear that one of these days you might accidentally die for one of them.

SEUMAS. You're one of the brave fellows that doesn't fear death.

DAVOREN. Why should I be afraid of it? It's all the same to me how it comes, where it comes or when it comes. I leave fear of death to the people that are always praying for eternal life; "Death is here and death is there, death is busy everywhere".

SEUMAS. Ay, in Ireland. Thanks be to God I'm a daily communicant. There's a great comfort in religion; it makes a man strong in time of trouble an' brave in time of

danger.   No man need be afraid with a crowd
of angels round him; thanks to God for His
Holy religion!

DAVOREN. You're welcome to your angels;
philosophy is mine; philosophy that makes the
coward brave; the sufferer defiant; the weak
strong; the . . .

> (*A volley of shots is heard in a lane that
> runs parallel with the wall of the back-
> yard.   Religion and philosophy are
> forgotten in the violent fear of a nervous
> equality.*)

SEUMAS. Jesus, Mary an' Joseph, what's
that?

DAVOREN. My God, that's very close.

SEUMAS. Is there no Christianity at all left
in the country?

DAVOREN. Are we ever again going to know
what peace and security are?

SEUMAS. If this continues much longer I'll
be nothing but a galvanic battery o' shocks.

DAVOREN. It's dangerous to be in and it's
equally dangerous to be out.

SEUMAS. This is a dangerous spot to be in
with them windows; you couldn't tell the
minute a bullet ud come in through one of
them—through one of them, an' hit the—hit
the—an' hit the . . .

169

DAVOREN (*irritably*). Hit the what, man?

SEUMAS. The wall.

DAVOREN. Couldn't you say that at first without making a song about it.

SEUMAS (*suddenly*). I don't believe there's horses in the stable at all.

DAVOREN. Stable! What stable are you talking about?

SEUMAS. There's a stable at the back of the house with an entrance from the yard; it's used as a carpenter's shop. Didn't you often hear the peculiar noises at night? They give out that it's the horses shakin' their chains.

DAVOREN. And what is it?

SEUMAS. Oh, there I'll leave you!

DAVOREN. Surely you don't mean. . . .

SEUMAS. But I do mean it.

DAVOREN. You do mean what?

SEUMAS. I wouldn't—I wouldn't be surprised—wouldn't be surprised—surprised . . .

DAVOREN. Yes, yes, surprised—go on.

SEUMAS. I wouldn't be surprised if they were manufacturin' bombs there.

DAVOREN. My God, that's a pleasant contemplation! The sooner I'm on the run out of this house the better. How is it you never said anything about this before?

SEUMAS. Well — well, I didn't want — I didn't want to — to . . .

DAVOREN. You didn't want to what?

SEUMAS. I didn't want to frighten you.

DAVOREN (*sarcastically*). You're bloody kind!

(*A knock at the door; the voice of* MRS. GRIGSON *heard.*)

MRS. GRIGSON. Are you asleep, Mr. Shields?

SEUMAS. What the devil can she want at this hour of the night? (*To* MRS. GRIGSON) No, Mrs. Grigson, what is it?

MRS. GRIGSON (*opening the door and standing at the threshold. She is a woman about forty, but looks much older. She is one of the cave-dwellers of Dublin, living as she does in a tenement kitchen, to which only an occasional sickly beam of sunlight filters through a grating in the yard; the consequent general dimness of her abode has given her a habit of peering through half-closed eyes. She is slovenly dressed in an old skirt and bodice; her face is grimy, not because her habits are dirty — for, although she is untidy, she is a clean woman — but because of the smoky atmosphere of her room. Her hair is constantly falling over her face, which she is as frequently removing by rapid movements of her right hand*). He hasn't turned up yet, an' I'm stiff with the cold waitin' for him.

SEUMAS. Mr. Grigson, is it?

MRS. GRIGSON. Adolphus, Mr. Shields, after takin' his tea at six o'clock—no, I'm tellin' a lie—it was before six, for I remember the Angelus was ringin' out an' we sittin' at the table—after takin' his tea he went out for a breath o' fresh air, an' I haven't seen sign or light of him since. 'Clare to God me heart is up in me mouth, thinkin' he might be shot be the Black an' Tans.

SEUMAS. Aw, he'll be all right, Mrs. Grigson. You ought to go to bed an' rest yourself; it's always the worst that comes into a body's mind; go to bed, Mrs. Grigson, or you'll catch your death of cold.

MRS. GRIGSON. I'm afraid to go to bed, Mr. Shields, for I'm always in dread that some night or another, when he has a sup taken, he'll fall down the kitchen stairs an' break his neck. Not that I'd be any the worse if anything did happen to him, for you know the sort he is, Mr. Shields; sure he has me heart broke.

SEUMAS. Don't be downhearted, Mrs. Grigson; he may take a thought one of these days an' turn over a new leaf.

MRS. GRIGSON. Sorra leaf Adolphus 'll ever turn over, he's too far gone in the horns for that now. Sure no one ud mind him takin' a pint or two, if he'd stop at that, but he won't;

nothin' could fill him with beer, an' no matter how much he may have taken, when he's taken more he'll always say, " here's the first to-day ".

DAVOREN (*to* SEUMAS). Christ! Is she going to stop talking there all the night?

SEUMAS. 'Sh, she'll hear you; right enough, the man has the poor woman's heart broke.

DAVOREN. And because he has her heart broken, she's to have the privilege of breaking everybody else's.

MRS. GRIGSON. Mr. Shields.

SEUMAS. Yes?

MRS. GRIGSON. Do the insurance companies pay if a man is shot after curfew?

SEUMAS. Well, now, that's a thing I couldn't say, Mrs. Grigson.

MRS. GRIGSON (*plaintively*). Isn't he a terrible man to be takin' such risks, an' not knowin' what'll happen to him. He knows them. Societies only want an excuse to do people out of their money—is it after one, now, Mr. Shields?

SEUMAS. Aw, it must be after one, Mrs. Grigson.

MRS. GRIGSON (*emphatically*). Ah, then, if I was a young girl again I'd think twice before gettin' married. Whisht! There's somebody now — it's him, I know be the way he's fumblin'.

> (*She goes out a little way. Stumbling steps are heard in the hall.*)

MRS. GRIGSON (*outside*). Is that you, Dolphie, dear?

> (*After a few moments,* ADOLPHUS, *with* MRS. GRIGSON *holding his arm, stumbles into the room.*)

MRS. GRIGSON. Dolphie, dear, mind yourself.

ADOLPHUS (*he is a man of fifty-five, but looks, relatively, much younger than* MRS. GRIGSON. *His occupation is that of a solicitor's clerk. He has all the appearance of being well fed; and, in fact, he gets most of the nourishment,* MRS. GRIGSON *getting just enough to give her strength to do the necessary work of the household. On account of living most of his life out of the kitchen, his complexion is fresh, and his movements, even when sober, are livelier than those of his wife. He is comfortably dressed; heavy top-coat, soft trilby hat, a fancy coloured scarf about his neck, and he carries an umbrella*). I'm all right; do you see anything wrong with me?

MRS. GRIGSON. Of course you're all right, dear; there's no one mindin' you.

ADOLPHUS GRIGSON. Mindin' me, is it,

mindin' me? He'd want to be a good thing that ud mind me. There's a man here—a man, mind you, afraid av nothin'—not in this bloody house anyway.

MRS. GRIGSON (*imploringly*). Come on downstairs, Dolphie, dear; sure there's not one in the house ud say a word to you.

ADOLPHUS GRIGSON. Say a word to me, is it? He'd want to be a good thing that ud say anything to Dolphus Grigson. (*Loudly*) Is there any one wants to say anything to Dolphus Grigson? If there is, he's here—a man, too—there's no blottin' it out—a man.

MRS. GRIGSON. You'll wake everybody in the house; can't you speak quiet.

ADOLPHUS GRIGSON (*more loudly still*). What do I care for anybody in the house? Are they keepin' me; are they givin' me anthing? When they're keepin' Grigson it'll be time enough for them to talk. (*With a shout*) I can tell them Adolphus Grigson wasn't born in a bottle!

MRS. GRIGSON (*tearfully*). Why do you talk like that, dear; we all know you weren't born in a bottle.

ADOLPHUS GRIGSON. There's some of them in this house think that Grigson was born in a bottle.

175

DAVOREN (*to* SEUMAS). A most appropriate place for him to be born in.

MRS. GRIGSON. Come on down to bed, now, an' you can talk about them in the mornin'.

ADOLPHUS. I'll talk about them, now; do you think I'm afraid of them? Dolphus Grigson afraid av nothin', creepin' or walkin',— if there's any one in the house thinks he's fit to take a fall out av Adolphus Grigson, he's here—a man; they'll find that Grigson's no soft thing.

DAVOREN. Ah me, alas! Pain, pain ever, for ever.

MRS. GRIGSON. Dolphie, dear, poor Mr. Davoren wants to go to bed.

DAVOREN. Oh, she's terribly anxious about poor Mr. Davoren, all of a sudden.

ADOLPHUS (*stumbling towards* DAVOREN, *and holding out his hand*). Davoren! He's a man. Leave it there, mate. You needn't be afraid av Dolphus Grigson; there never was a drop av informer's blood in the whole family av Grigson. I don't know what you are or what you think, but you're a man, an' not like some of the goughers in this house, that ud hang you. Not referrin' to you, Mr. Shields.

MRS. GRIGSON. Oh, you're not deludin' to Mr. Shields.

SEUMAS. I know that, Mr. Grigson; go on down, now, with Mrs. Grigson, an' have a sleep.

ADOLPHUS. I tie meself to no woman's apron strings, Mr. Shields; I know how to keep Mrs. Grigson in her place; I have the authority of the Bible for that. I know the Bible from cover to cover, Mr. Davoren, an' that's more than some in this house could say. And what does the Holy Scripture say about woman? It says, " The woman shall be subject to her husband," an' I'll see that Mrs. Grigson keeps the teachin' av the Holy Book in the letter an' in the spirit. If you're ever in trouble, Mr. Davoren, an' Grigson can help—I'm your man—have you me?

DAVOREN. I have you, Mr. Grigson, I have you.

GRIGSON. Right; I'm an Orangeman, an' I'm not ashamed av it, an' I'm not afraid av it, but I can feel for a true man, all the same— have *you* got me, Mr. Shields?

SEUMAS. Oh, we know you well, Mr. Grigson; many a true Irishman was a Protestant—Tone, Emmet an' Parnell.

ADOLPHUS GRIGSON. Mind you, I'm not sayin' as I agree with them you've mentioned, Mr. Shields, for the Bible forbids it, an' Adolphus Grigson 'll always abide be the Bible.

Fear God an' honour the King—that's written in Holy Scripture, an' there's no blottin' it out. (*Pulling a bottle out of his pocket*) But, here, Mr. Davoren, have a drink, just to show there's no coolness.

DAVOREN. No, no, Mr. Grigson, it's too late now to take anything. Go on down with Mrs. Grigson, and we can have a chat in the morning.

ADOLPHUS GRIGSON. Sure you won't have a drink?

DAVOREN. Quite sure—thanks all the same.

ADOLPHUS GRIGSON (*drinking*). Here's the first to-day! To all true men, even if they were born in a bottle. Here's to King William, to the battle av the Boyne; to the Hobah Black Chapter—that's my Lodge, Mr. Davoren; an' to The Orange Lily O. (*Singing in a loud shout*):

An' dud ya go to see the show, each rose an' pinka-
    dilly O,
To feast your eyes an' view the prize won be the
    Orange Lily O.
The Vic'roy there, so debonair, just like a daffadilly O,
With Lady Clarke, blithe as a lark, approached the
    Orange Lily O.
           Heigh Ho the Lily O,
           The Royal, Loyal Lily O,
Beneath the sky what flower can vie with Erin's
    Orange Lily O.

DAVOREN. Holy God, isn't this terrible!
GRIGSON (*singing*):

The elated Muse, to hear the news, jumped like a
    Connaught filly O,
As gossip Fame did loud proclaim, the triumph av the
    Lily O.
The Lowland field may roses yield, gay heaths the
    Highlands hilly O;
But high or low no flower can show like Erin's Orange
    Lily O.
            Heigh Ho the Lily O,
            The Royal, Loyal Lily O,
Beneath the sky what flower can vie with Erin's
    Or . . .

> (*While* GRIGSON *has been singing the
> sound of a rapidly moving motor is heard
> faintly at first, but growing rapidly
> louder, till it apparently stops suddenly
> somewhere very near the house, bringing*
> GRIGSON'S *song to an abrupt conclusion.
> They are all startled, and listen atten-
> tively to the throbbing of the engines,
> which can be plainly heard.* GRIGSON
> *is considerably sobered, and anxiously
> keeps his eyes on the door.* SEUMAS *sits
> up in the bed and listens anxiously.*
> DAVOREN, *with a shaking hand, lights
> the candle, and begins to search hurriedly*

179

among the books and papers on the table.)

ADOLPHUS GRIGSON (*with a tremor in his voice*). There's no need to be afraid, they couldn't be comin' here.

MRS. GRIGSON. God forbid! It ud be terrible if they came at this hour ov the night.

SEUMAS. You never know now, Mrs. Grigson; they'd rush in on you when you'd be least expectin' them. What, in the name o' God, is goin' to come out of it all? Nobody now cares a traneen about the orders of the Ten Commandments; the only order that anybody minds now is, " put your hands up ". Oh, it's a hopeless country.

ADOLPHUS GRIGSON. Whisht; do you hear them talking outside at the door? You're sure of your life nowhere now; it's just as safe to go everywhere as it is to anywhere. An' they don't give a damn whether you're a loyal man or not. If you're a Republican they make you sing " God save the King ", an' if you're loyal they'll make you sing the " Soldiers' Song ". The singin' ud be all right if they didn't make you dance afterwards.

MRS. GRIGSON. They'd hardly come here unless they heard something about Mr. Davoren.

DAVOREN. About me! What could they hear about me?

ADOLPHUS GRIGSON. You'll never get some people to keep their mouths shut. I was in the Blue Lion this evening, an' who do you think was there, blowin' out av him, but that little blower, Tommy Owens; there he was tellin' everybody that *he* knew where there was bombs; that *he* had a friend that was a General in the I.R.A.; that *he* could tell them what the Staff was thinkin' av doin'; that *he* could lay his hand on tons av revolvers; that they wasn't a mile from where he was livin', but that *he* knew his own know, an' would keep it to himself.

SEUMAS. Well, God blast the little blower, anyway; it's the like ov him that deserves to be plugged! (*To* DAVOREN) What are you lookin' for among the books, Donal?

DAVOREN. A letter that I got to-day from Mr. Gallogher and Mrs. Henderson; I'm blessed if I know where I put it.

SEUMAS (*peevishly*). Can't you look for it in the mornin'?

DAVOREN. It's addressed to the Irish Republican Army, and, considering the possibility of a raid, it would be safer to get rid of it.

*(Shots again heard out in the lane, followed
by loud shouts of Halt, halt, halt!)*

ADOLPHUS GRIGSON. I think we had better
be gettin' to bed, Debby; it's not right to be
keepin' Mr. Davoren an' Mr. Shields awake.

SEUMAS. An' what made them give you such
a letter as that; don't they know the state the
country is in? An' you were worse to take it.
Have you got it?

DAVOREN. I can't find it anywhere; isn't
this terrible!

ADOLPHUS GRIGSON. Good-night, Mr.
Davoren; good-night, Mr. Shields.

MRS. GRIGSON. Good-night, Mr. Shields;
good-night, Mr. Davoren.

*(They go out.   SEUMAS and DAVOREN are
too much concerned about the letter to
respond to their good-nights.)*

SEUMAS. What were you thinkin' of when
you took such a letter as that? Ye gods, has
nobody any brains at all, at all? Oh, this is a
hopeless country. Did you try in your pockets?

DAVOREN *(searching in his pockets)*. Oh,
thanks be to God, here it is.

SEUMAS. Burn it now, an', for God's sake,
don't take any letters like that again. . . .
There's the motor goin' away; we can sleep
in peace now for the rest of the night. Just

to make sure of everything now, have a look in that bag o' Maguire's: not that there can be anything in it.

DAVOREN. If there's nothing in it what's the good of looking?

SEUMAS. It won't kill you to look, will it?

(DAVOREN *goes over to the bag, puts it on the table, opens it, and jumps back, his face pale and his limbs trembling.*)

DAVOREN. My God, it's full of bombs, Mills bombs!

SEUMAS. Holy Mother of God, you're jokin'!

DAVOREN. If the Tans come you'll find whether I'm jokin' or no.

SEUMAS. Isn't this a nice pickle to be in? St. Anthony, look down on us!

DAVOREN. There's no use of blaming St. Anthony; why did you let Maguire leave the bag here?

SEUMAS. Why did I let him leave the bag here; why did I let him leave the bag here! How did I know what was in it? Didn't I think there was nothin' in it but spoons an' hairpins. What'll we do now; what'll we do now? Mother o' God, grant there'll be no raid to-night. I knew things ud go wrong when I missed Mass this mornin'.

DAVOREN. Give over your praying and let

183

us try to think of what is best to be done.
There's one thing certain: as soon as morning
comes I'm on the run out of this house.

SEUMAS. Thinkin' of yourself, like the rest
of them. Leavin' me to bear the brunt of it.

DAVOREN. And why shouldn't you bear the
brunt of it? Maguire was no friend of mine;
besides it's your fault; you knew the sort of a
man he was, and you should have been on your
guard.

SEUMAS. Did I know he was a gunman; did
I know he was a gunman; did I know he was
a gunman? Did . . .

DAVOREN. Do you mean to tell me that . . .

SEUMAS. Just a moment . . .

DAVOREN. You didn't know . . .

SEUMAS. Just a moment . . .

DAVOREN. That Maguire was connected
with . . .

SEUMAS (*loudly*). Just a moment; can't . . .

DAVOREN. The Republican Movement?
What's the use of trying to tell damn lies!

(MINNIE POWELL *rushes into the room.*
She is only partly dressed, and has
thrown a shawl over her shoulders. She
is in a state of intense excitement.)

MINNIE. Mr. Davoren, Donal, they're all
round the house; they must be goin' to raid

the place; I was lookin' out of the window an' I seen them; I do be on the watch every night; have you anything?   If you have . . .

> (*There is heard at street door a violent and continuous knocking, followed by the crash of glass and the beating of the door with rifle butts.*)

MINNIE. There they are, there they are, there they are!

> (DAVOREN *reclines almost fainting on the bed;* SEUMAS *sits up in an attitude of agonized prayerfulness;* MINNIE *alone retains her presence of mind. When she sees their panic she becomes calm, though her words are rapidly spoken, and her actions are performed with decisive celerity.*)

MINNIE. What is it; what have you got; where are they?

DAVOREN. Bombs, bombs, bombs; my God! in the bag on the table there; we're done, we're done!

SEUMAS. Hail Mary full of grace—pray for us miserable sinners—Holy St. Anthony, do you hear them batterin' at the door—now an' at the hour of our death—say an act of contrition, Donal—there's the glass gone!

MINNIE. I'll take them to my room; maybe

they won't search it; if they do aself, they won't harm a girl.   Good-bye . . . Donal.

> (*She glances lovingly at* DONAL—*who is only semi-conscious—as she rushes out with the bag.*)

SEUMAS. If we come through this I'll never miss a Mass again!   If it's the Tommies it won't be so bad, but if it's the Tans, we're goin' to have a terrible time.

> (*The street door is broken open and heavy steps are heard in the hall, punctuated with shouts of* "'*Old the light 'ere*", "*Put 'em up*", *etc.   An* AUXILIARY *opens the door of the room and enters, revolver in one hand and electric torch in the other.*)

THE AUXILIARY. 'Oo's 'ere?

SEUMAS (*as if he didn't know*). Who—who's that?

THE AUXILIARY (*peremptorily*). 'Oo's 'ere?

SEUMAS. Only two men, mister; me an' me mate in t'other bed.

THE AUXILIARY. Why didn't you open the door?

SEUMAS. We didn't hear you knockin', sir.

THE AUXILIARY. You must be a little awd of 'earing, ay?

SEUMAS. I had rheumatic fever a few years

ago, an' ever since I do be a—I do be a little deaf sometimes.

THE AUXILIARY (*to* DAVOREN). 'Ow is it you're not in bed?

DAVOREN. I was in bed; when I heard the knockin' I got up to open the door.

THE AUXILIARY. *You're* a koind blowke, you are.   Deloighted, like, to have a visit from us, ay? Ay? (*Threatening to strike him*) Why down't you answer?

DAVOREN. Yes, sir.

THE AUXILIARY. What's your name?

DAVOREN. Davoren, Dan Davoren, sir.

THE AUXILIARY. You're not an Irishman, are you?

DAVOREN. I-I-I was born in Ireland.

THE AUXILIARY. Ow, you were, were you; Irish han' proud of it, ay?   (*To* SEUMAS) What's *your* name?

SEUMAS. Seuma . . . Oh no; Jimmie Shields, sir.

THE AUXILIARY. Ow, you're a selt (*he means a Celt*), one of the seltic race that speaks a lingo of its ahn, and that's going to overthrow the British Empire—I don't think!   'Ere, where's your gun?

SEUMAS. I never had a gun in me hand in me life.

THE AUXILIARY. Now; you wouldn't know what a gun is if you sawr one, I suppowse. (*Displaying his revolver in a careless way*) 'Ere, what's that?

SEUMAS. Oh, be careful, please, be careful.

THE AUXILIARY. Why; what 'ave I got to be careful abaht?

SEUMAS. The gun; it-it-it might go off.

THE AUXILIARY. An' what prawse if it did; it can easily be relowded. Any ammunition 'ere? What's in that press? (*He searches and scatters contents of press.*)

SEUMAS. Only a little bit o' grub; you'll get nothin' here, sir; no one in the house has any connection with politics.

THE AUXILIARY. Now? I've never met a man yet that didn't say that, but we're a little bit too ikey now to be kidded with that sort of talk.

SEUMAS. May I go an' get a drink o' water?

THE AUXILIARY. Yoy'll want a barrel of watah before you're done with us. (THE AUXILIARY *goes about the room examining places*) 'Ello, what's 'ere? A statue o' Christ! An' a Crucifix! You'd think you was in a bloomin' monastery.

(MRS. GRIGSON *enters, dressed disorderly and her hair awry.*)

188

MRS. GRIGSON. They're turning the place upside down. Upstairs an' downstairs they're makin' a litter of everything! I declare to God, it's awful what law-abidin' people have to put up with. An' they found a pint bottle of whisky under Dolphie's pillow, an' they're drinkin' every drop of it—an' Dolphie 'll be like a devil in the mornin' when he finds he has no curer.

THE AUXILIARY (*all attention when he hears the word whisky*). A bottle of whisky, ay? 'Ere, where do you live—quick, where do you live?

MRS. GRIGSON. Down in the kitchen—an' when you go down will you ask them not to drink—oh, he's gone without listenin' to me.

(*While* MRS. GRIGSON *is speaking* THE AUXILIARY *rushes out*.)

SEUMAS (*anxiously to* MRS. GRIGSON). Are they searchin' the whole house, Mrs. Grigson?

MRS. GRIGSON. They didn't leave a thing in the kitchen that they didn't flitter about the floor; the things in the cupboard, all the little odds an' ends that I keep in the big box, an . . .

SEUMAS. Oh, they're a terrible gang of blaguards—did they go upstairs?—they'd hardly search Minnie Powell's room—do you think would they, Mrs. Grigson?

189

MRS. GRIGSON. Just to show them the sort
of a man he was, before they come in, Dolphie
put the big Bible on the table, open at the
First Gospel of St. Peter, second chapter, an'
marked the thirteenth to the seventeenth verse
in red ink—you know the passages, Mr. Shields
—(*quoting*):

" Submit yourselves to every ordinance of man for
the Lord's sake: whether it be to the king, as supreme;
or unto governors, as unto them that are sent by him
for the punishment of evildoers, an' for the praise of
them that do well. . . . Love the brotherhood.   Fear
God.   Honour the King."

An' what do you think they did, Mr. Shields?
They caught a hold of the Bible an' flung it
on the floor—imagine that, Mr. Shields—
flingin' the Bible on the floor!   Then one of
them says to another—" Jack," says he, " have
you seen the light; is your soul saved?"   An'
then they grabbed hold of poor Dolphie, callin'
him Mr. Moody an' Mr. Sankey, an' wanted
him to offer up a prayer for the Irish Republic!
An' when they were puttin' me out, there they
had the poor man sittin' up in bed, his hands
crossed on his breast, his eyes lookin' up at
the ceilin', an' he singin' a hymn—" We shall
meet in the Sweet Bye an' Bye "—an' all the
time, Mr. Shields, there they were drinkin' his

whisky; there's torture for you, an' they all laughin' at poor Dolphie's terrible sufferins.

DAVOREN. In the name of all that's sensible, what did he want to bring whisky home with him for? They're bad enough sober, what'll they be like when they're drunk?

MRS. GRIGSON (*plaintively*). He always brings a drop home with him—he calls it his medicine.

SEUMAS (*still anxious*). They'll hardly search all the house; do you think they will, Mrs. Grigson?

MRS. GRIGSON. An' we have a picture over the mantelpiece of King William crossing the Boyne, an' do you know what they wanted to make out, Mr. Shields, that it was Robert Emmet, an' the picture of a sacret society!

SEUMAS. She's not listenin' to a word I'm sayin'! Oh, the country is hopeless an' the people is hopeless.

DAVOREN. For God's sake tell her to go to hell out of this—she's worse than the Auxsie.

SEUMAS (*thoughtfully*). Let her stay where she is; it's safer to have a woman in the room. If they come across the bombs I hope to God Minnie 'll say nothin'.

DAVOREN. We're a pair of pitiable cowards to let poor Minnie suffer when we know that we and not she are to blame.

SEUMAS. What else can we do, man? Do you want us to be done in? If you're anxious to be riddled, I'm not. Besides, they won't harm her, she's only a girl, an' so long as she keeps her mouth shut it'll be all right.

DAVOREN. I wish I could be sure of that.

SEUMAS. D'ye think are they goin', Mrs. Grigson? What are they doin' now?

MRS. GRIGSON (*who is standing at the door, looking out into the hall*). There's not a bit of me that's not shakin' like a jelly!

SEUMAS. Are they gone upstairs, Mrs. Grigson? Do you think, Mrs. Grigson, will they soon be goin'?

MRS. GRIGSON. When they were makin' poor Dolphie sit up in the bed, I 'clare to God I thought every minute I'd hear their guns goin' off, an' see poor Dolphie stretched out dead in the bed—whisht, God bless us, I think I hear him moanin'!

SEUMAS. You might as well be talking to a stone! They're all hopeless, hopeless, hopeless! She thinks she hears him moanin'! It's bloody near time somebody made him moan!

DAVOREN (*with a sickly attempt at humour*). He's moaning for the loss of his whisky.

(*During the foregoing dialogue the various sounds of a raid—orders, the tramping of heavy feet, the pulling about of furniture, etc., are heard. Now a more definite and sustained commotion is apparent. Loud and angry commands of " Go on ", " Get out and get into the lorry ", are heard, mingled with a girl's voice—it is* MINNIE'S—*shouting bravely, but a little hysterically, " Up the Republic ".)*

MRS. GRIGSON (*from the door*). God save us, they're takin' Minnie, they're takin' Minnie Powell! (*Running out*) What in the name of God can have happened?

SEUMAS. Holy Saint Anthony grant that she'll keep her mouth shut.

DAVOREN (*sitting down on the bed and covering his face with his hands*). We'll never again be able to lift up our heads if anything happens to Minnie.

SEUMAS. For God's sake keep quiet or somebody'll hear you; nothin'll happen to her, nothin' at all—it'll be all right if she only keeps her mouth shut.

MRS. GRIGSON (*running in*). They're after gettin' a whole lot of stuff in Minnie's room! Enough to blow up the whole street, a Tan says! God to-night, who'd have ever thought that of Minnie Powell!

SEUMAS. Did she say anything, is she sayin' anything, what's she sayin', Mrs. Grigson?

MRS. GRIGSON. She's shoutin' "Up the Republic" at the top of her voice. An' big Mrs. Henderson is fightin' with the soldiers— she's after nearly knockin' one of them down, an' they're puttin' her into the lorry too.

SEUMAS. God blast her! Can she not mind her own business? What does she want here —didn't she know there was a raid on? Is the whole damn country goin' mad? They'll open fire in a minute an' innocent people'll be shot!

DAVOREN. What way are they using Minnie, Mrs. Grigson; are they rough with her?

MRS. GRIGSON. They couldn't be half rough enough; the little hussy, to be so deceitful; she might as well have had the house blew up! God to-night, who'd think it was in Minnie Powell!

SEUMAS. Oh, grant she won't say anything!

MRS. GRIGSON. There they're goin' away, now; ah, then I hope they'll give that Minnie Powell a coolin'.

SEUMAS. God grant she won't say anything! Are they gone, Mrs. Grigson?

MRS. GRIGSON. With her fancy stockins, an' her pom-poms, an' her crêpe de chine blouses! I knew she'd come to no good!

SEUMAS. God grant she'll keep her mouth shut! Are they gone, Mrs. Grigson?

MRS. GRIGSON. They're gone, Mr. Shields, an' here's poor Dolphie an' not a feather astray on him. Oh, Dolphie, dear, you're all right, thanks to God; I thought you'd never see the mornin'.

GRIGSON (*entering without coat or vest*). Of course I'm all right; what ud put a bother on Dolphie Grigson?—not the Tans anyway!

MRS. GRIGSON. When I seen you stretched out on the bed, an' you . . . singin' a hymn . . .

MR. GRIGSON (*fearful of possible humiliation*). Who was singin' a hymn? When did you hear me singin' a hymn? D'ye hear me talkin' to you—where did you hear me singin' a hymn?

MRS. GRIGSON. I was only jokin', Dolphie, dear; I . . .

MR. GRIGSON. You're place is below, an' not gosterin' here to men; down with you quick!

(MRS. GRIGSON *hurriedly leaves the room.*)

MR. GRIGSON (*nonchalantly taking out his pipe, filling it, lighting it, and beginning to smoke*). Excitin' few moments, Mr. Davoren; Mrs. G. lost her head completely—panic-stricken. But that's only natural, all women is very nervous.

195

The only thing to do is to show them that they can't put the wind up you; show the least sign of fright an' they'd walk on you, simply walk on you. Two of them come down— " Put them up " revolvers under your nose— you know, the usual way. " What's all the bother about? " says I, quite calm. " No bother at all," says one of them, " only this gun might go off an' hit somebody—have you me? " says he. " What if it does," says I, " a man can only die once, an' you'll find Grigson won't squeal." " God, you're a cool one," says the other, " there's no blottin' it out."

SEUMAS. That's the best way to take them; it only makes things worse to show that you've got the wind up. " Any ammunition here? " says the fellow that come in here. " I don't think so," says I, " but you better have a look." " No back talk," says he, " or you might get plugged." " I don't know of any clause," says I, " in the British Constitution that makes it a crime for a man to speak in his own room,"—with that, he just had a look round, an' off he went.

MR. GRIGSON. If a man keeps a stiff upper front—Merciful God, there's an ambush!

(*Explosions of two bursting bombs are*

heard on the street outside the house, followed by fierce and rapid revolver and rifle fire. People are heard rushing into the hall, and there is general clamour and confusion. SEUMAS *and* DAVOREN *cower down in the room;* GRIGSON, *after a few moments' hesitation, frankly rushes out of the room to what he conceives to be the safer asylum of the kitchen. A lull follows, punctuated by an odd rifle-shot; then comes a peculiar and ominous stillness, broken in a few moments by the sounds of voices and movement. Questions are heard being asked:* " *Who was it was killed?* " " *Where was she shot?* " *which are answered by* " MINNIE POWELL "; " *She went to jump off the lorry an' she was shot.* " " *She's not dead, is she?* " " *They say she's dead —shot through the buzzum!* ")

DAVOREN (*in a tone of horror-stricken doubt*). D'ye hear what they're sayin', Shields, d'ye hear what they're sayin'?—Minnie Powell is shot.

SEUMAS. For God's sake speak easy, an' don't bring them in here on top of us again.

DAVOREN. Is that all you're thinking of?

197

Do you realize that she has been shot to save us?

SEUMAS. Is it my fault; am I to blame?

DAVOREN. It is your fault and mine, both; oh, we're a pair of dastardly cowards to have let her do what she did.

SEUMAS. She did it off her own bat—we didn't ask her to do it.

(MRS. GRIGSON *enters.* *She is excited and semi-hysterical, and sincerely affected by the tragic occurrence.*)

MRS. GRIGSON (*falling down in a sitting posture on one of the beds*). What's goin' to happen next! Oh, Mr. Davoren, isn't it terrible, isn't it terrible! Minnie Powell, poor little Minnie Powell's been shot dead! They were raidin' a house a few doors down, an' had just got up in their lorries to go away when they was ambushed. You never heard such shootin'! An' in the thick of it, poor Minnie went to jump off the lorry she was on, an' she was shot through the buzzum. Oh, it was horrible to see the blood pourin' out, an' Minnie moanin'. They found some paper in her breast, with "Minnie" written on it, an' some other name they couldn't make out with the blood; the officer kep' it. The ambulance is bringin' her to the hospital, but what good's that when she's dead! Poor little Minnie, poor little Minnie Powell, to think of you full of life a few minutes ago, an' now she's dead!

DAVOREN. Ah me, alas! Pain, pain, pain ever, for ever! It's terrible to think that little Minnie is dead, but it's still more terrible to think that Davoren and Shields are alive! Oh, Donal Davoren, shame is your portion now till the silver cord is loosened and the golden bowl be broken. Oh, Davoren, Donal Davoren, poet and poltroon, poltroon and poet!

SEUMAS (*solemnly*). I knew something ud come of the tappin' on the wall!

CURTAIN

Printed in Great Britain by R. & R. CLARK, LIMITED, *Edinburgh*